SANTA FE ON FOOT

SANTA FE ON FOOT

Walking, Running and Bicycling Routes in the City Different

BY ELAINE PINKERTON

Illustrated by Eli Levin

Ocean Tree / Cota Edition   *Santa Fe*

Distributed in New Mexico by:
>Juniper Junction
>899 Zia Road
>Santa Fe, New Mexico 87505

Published nationally by:
>Ocean Tree Services
>Post Office Box 1295
>Santa Fe, New Mexico 87504

Edited by Richard Polese
Original drawings by Eli Levin
Book design and maps by Louann Jordan
Production by Ocean Tree Services
IBSN: 0-943734-05-3
Library of Congress Catalog Card: 86-060510

ACKNOWLEDGEMENTS

The ideas for *SANTA FE ON FOOT* are the natural outgrowth of nearly twenty years in Santa Fe, and of my love of walking, running and bicycling. However, without the assistance of Richard Polese, my editor, these ideas might never have evolved into a book. His enthusiasm, attention to detail and patience have been invaluable.

Others who have shared their knowledge of Santa Fe include: Dr. Myra Ellen Jenkins, Marc Simmons, Orlando Romero, James Purdy, Jerry Porter, Mary Helen Follingstad, Jane Petchesky, Dr. Robert Derbyshire, Louie Ewing, Catherine Rayne, Jan Rhodes and Harry Moul. For the running section of the book, Dede Collins, Jim Rubin and Louis Pisano provided important information. The Sisters of the Blessed Sacrament at St. Catherine Indian School were most helpful. I would also like to thank Leo Schlachter, who acted as my bicycling consultant, and Linda Aldrich of the Los Alamos Historical Society. To these individuals, and to the many others who so generously gave of their time, my sincere gratitude.

For Robert H. Dinegar,
with love and appreciation.

CONTENTS

INTRODUCTION

The Plaza, heart of Santa Fe

The reason for *SANTA FE ON FOOT* is simple. I would like to introduce you to the joys of walking, running and bicycling, or if you already appreciate these activities, to increase and broaden that enjoyment in a fascinating city. I would like to offer you a unique view of Santa Fe's culture and natural setting. Running and walking are good for people. Add to their physical benefits the goal of seeing Santa Fe with a fresh look, and you have a combination which doubly rewards. You may have lived in Santa Fe for years, or you may just be visiting, but until you have toured it on foot, you've never really seen it.

SANTA FE ON FOOT has been four years in the writing. My walking and running research began much earlier. I came to Santa Fe in the mid-1960s, but it wasn't until moving away and then back a decade later that I began to love Santa Fe outdoors.

I joined a hiking group. Every Friday, we would pack up our gear and head for the mountains. We hiked to Spirit Lake, Penitente Peak, Lake Catherine, Santa Fe Baldy, Tetilla Peak, to ghost towns and lost canyons, to sacred Indian shrines and obscure petroglyph sites. On winter days when the weather was too threatening to travel anywhere out of town, we would "walk Santa Fe," passing familiar sights but taking the time for an in-depth view.

One particularly cold, snowy winter day, we walked along the railroad tracks for a Santa Fe seldom seen. There were wandering hobos, a few people living in derelict school buses, and a lonely "on the road" feeling in the atmosphere. Later in the morning we visited Josie's Tortilla Factory and bought hot, fresh tortillas to eat on the spot. We stopped at the Institute of American Indian Arts museum. By the end of the day, it seemed like we had covered far more than eight miles. Our purposeful wandering had been a mini-vacation. Time had taken on a different meaning.

The hiking group eventually dissolved, and I became devoted to daily running. I went quickly from a mile to five, then to a half-marathon and a full marathon distances. In three years of competitive running, I was in many road races and nine marathons. And I discovered that running, as well as walking, was a great way to explore on foot.

Walking is advocated as a healthy activity by every authority these days, but running, it seems, has taken a beating from recent publicity. Some doctors are warning that there are more risks involved with running than originally perceived. Others are downright opposed to the activity. Frankly, I'm skeptical. Many people continue to benefit from running. The key to safety is moderation and suitability. But what is moderate for one person may be extreme for another. Age, general condition, and athletic background are factors. If you're in doubt about whether or not you should run, use common sense and build up gradually. Check with your doctor and take your own exercise history into consideration. Any of the running routes recommended in *SANTA FE ON FOOT* can also be walked, and vice versa.

A few words of warning: When you exercise in Santa Fe, remember that its high altitude will probably alter your capabilities. Coming from sea level to 7,000 feet, you'll most certainly find yourself tiring earlier than usual. Instead of being able to run five miles, you may need to limit yourself to three. On walks, you might want to take longer breaks. Most people do adjust to the altitude in a few days, but don't be surprised if you need to take afternoon siestas when you first arrive. Follow your natural inclinations. St. Vincent Hospital's emergency room is set up to treat symptoms of anoxia (low oxygen level), but if you stop exercising before you get into difficulty, such a visit will never be necessary.

For women especially, it is important never to run or walk alone in isolated areas. Be careful at dawn and dusk. Though Santa Fe retains much of its small town ambiance, it does, unfortunately, have many crime problems of the big city.

It's easier to sunburn at Santa Fe's elevation. Always apply protective lotion to your face, arms and legs. Wear sunglasses or a hat with a brim.

If you are not acquainted with the magic of travelling by foot, trying the routes in this book just might transform you into an advocate. We're in an age of getting back to the basics. Organic foods, natural fabrics, herbal medicine and alternative methods of healing all abound (especially in Santa Fe), so it is not surprising that the "primitive" modes, walking, running and bicycling, are also gaining popularity. In societies where lots of foot travel is a necessity, people are freer from heart disease and other degenerative ailments. Even in America of fifty years ago, when people most often walked to work, school and social events, as well as up and down the stories of houses, sufficient walking each day helped maintain fitness. Obesity and its accompanying diseases were not the rule. Technology had not made vigorous living obsolete. The benefits of this natural exercise were taken for granted.

In our society, it seems almost as though walking is a luxury and jogging, a primarily middle-class activity, a "privilege." Most of us no longer need to use our legs to cover territory. Perhaps in the manner of the white hunter who stalks Africa in search of game, or the English poets who walked for miles and days to dream, compose and create, we've had to invent other goals to get us out again on the roads and trails.

For me, the beauty of travel by foot is very simply its closeness to nature. I am a mountain worshipper, and I love Santa Fe's skies. I'm also beginning to appreciate the wealth of its history.

When you travel historic areas, you can discover them more throroughly by foot than ever possible by car. When encountering something of particular fascination along the route, you're free to meander and tarry, to explore in depth. Another very real benefit is a sort of gaining time by losing it. The usual responsibilities take a back seat when you're out on foot. No phones can interrupt your mental relaxation. Nor are you limited by the time left on a parking meter. In Wordsworthian fashion, you can store up visions of Santa Fe's natural beauty for later use.

Lace up your road shoes, throw a few simple supplies in a pack, and go discover this wonderful city for yourself!

Elaine Pinkerton
Santa Fe, New Mexico

THE SANTA FE BACKGROUND

Past and Present

The Farmer's Market, a summer event held off Montezuma Street in Sanbusco Center.

Entire libraries are devoted to the history of Santa Fe and New Mexico, and my book isn't intended to be a history. However, I realize that one can hardly talk about Santa Fe without delving into its past. Santa Fe is living history. As you walk about the town and countryside of America's oldest capital city, you will encounter the major trade route of the old West, institutions established during the country's tuberculosis epidemic, a famous art colony, colleges and schools developed in the sixties, a major rodeo, historic homes and landmarks, and more. I'll try here to give you an overview of how Santa Fe grew to be what it is today.

Coming to Santa Fe is truly coming to another world. There isn't another city in the United States that excells Santa Fe in romance and history. Narrow, old-world streets lined with reddish-brown adobe houses with picturesque patios, the towering cottonwoods, the fragrance of pinon smoke, the music of spoken Spanish, the colorful appearance of Indians from the neighboring Pueblos—all these are part of Santa Fe's beauty and fascination. In this century, Santa Fe became a mecca for artists, writers, musicians and craftspeople, producing works of the highest quality. Opera and theatre flourish in this city of 60,000, a state capital that was called by one writer "America's Salzburg". Santa Fe of the 1980s is, among other things, an elite oasis of fame, big money and high culture. And yet the elements which drew people to Santa Fe in the first place remain.

THE PAST

New Mexico's known prehistory dates back to 12,000 B.C. In southern and western New Mexico, early cave dwellers hunted and gathered. By 1300 A.D., the Pueblos were well-established. Some of them, such as Taos Pueblo, exist to this day. In 1539, around the time of Michaelangelo's *The Last Judgement*, three shipwrecked Spaniards and a Moorish slave reached New Spain (today's Mexico) and heard legends of the "Seven Cities of Cibola". Their expeditions north found not golden cities but mud villages. Throughout the 1540s, aspiring conquistador Francisco Vasques de Coronado led quests for the fabled cities.

In 1595 Juan de Onate was given authority by Spain to colonize what by now was named *"Nuevo Mexico"*. In 1598, the first major colonizing expedition of Spaniards arrived along the Rio Grande. It included 129 families, 10 Franciscan friars, 700 Mexican Indians, many head of livestock, seeds and supplies. One man's sole responsibility was to count the paces of the entire journey from Mexico. Villagra, considered to be New Mexico's first historian, was part of this expedition.

Onate established the first settlement of New Mexico at San Gabriel, near the present San Juan Pueblo, 25 miles north of Santa Fe. From this base, the Franciscans set out to convert the Pueblos. Between 1600 and 1625, fifty churches were built.

In the year 1610, Don Pedro de Peralta, the third governor of New Mexico, moved the capital to Santa Fe. This fact makes it the oldest capital in the United States. The original source for its name was probably Santa Fe de Granada in Spain. The official name that Santa Fe now bears, *La Villa de la Santa Fe de San Francisco de Asis,* actually came in 1823, when St. Francis was adopted as the city's patron saint. The site of Santa Fe was originally a Pueblo Indian village. The area, according to legend, was called "the dancing ground of the Sun."

In the same year Santa Fe was established, the Palace of the Governors was constructed, as were the Chapel of San Miguel and a mission church. The first 70 years of Spanish rule were tumultuous. There was constant disagreement between civil and religious authorities, and the Pueblos suffered under sometimes brutal repression of their traditional ways. In 1680, the Indians rebelled and the Spanish were forced to flee south to El Paso del Norte (now Juarez, Mexico). For 13 years the Indians occupied Santa Fe. Part of the Palace of the Governors was transformed into a *kiva* and Indian headquarters.

In 1692, Governor-General Don Diego de Vargas made a reconnaissance and the next year reconquered New Mexico and returned Santa Fe to Spanish hands. Relations between Spanish and Indians improved, largely because the religious practices of the Pueblos were tolerated by their new conquerors. During this period, Santa Fe, and New Mexico, were practically isolated from the rest of the world. Spain allowed no foreign trade, and the lumbering *carretas* (wagons) carrying goods to and from Mexico along the Chihuahua Trail arrived infrequently in Santa Fe. This isolation was a major factor in developing the distinctive New Mexican culture, including weaving and religious art so prized by collectors today.

Santa Fe's centuries of isolation came to an end in 1822 when William Becknell brought wagonloads of goods into the city from Missouri, opening the famous Santa Fe Trail. As a result of the Louisiana Purchase, a new breed of men had begun moving westward— Americans who would not be kept out of New Mexico by Spain's restrictive trade policies. Further South there was a new passion for independence from Spain. But even though New Mexico, as part of Mexico, became independent from Spain in 1821, the Spanish influence brought by those early settlers and explorers still holds its grip on Santa Fe. Mexican control of

New Mexico lasted just 25 years.

When General Stephen Watts Kearny and his troops came to Santa Fe in 1846 to raise the Stars and Stripes, a new era began. The U.S. had declared war on Mexico and swept through the West, fulfilling the "Manifest Destiny" spirit to extend American sovereignty to the Pacific. Yet Kearny respected the established customs of the Spanish and Indian inhabitants of New Mexico, and the transition to American territorial status came fairly easily.

THE ANCIENT CHURCHES

It has been said that Santa Fe's churches accurately reflect its past, and we see this is true when we examine the history of San Miguel Chapel and the other Catholic churches in town. The church always has and still does play a central role in the life of Santa Fe's Hispanic population, descendents of the original conquerors.

When General de Vargas regained possession of the City of Holy Faith in 1693, he found its churches in a sorry state. He established a chapel in the Palace of the Governors. A parish church (*La Parroquia*) was built on the east side of the Plaza and San Miguel Chapel was restored on its original site. It is interesting to note that archaelogical excavations made at San Miguel in 1955, at the request of the Christian Brothers, revealed that more extensive rebuilding had taken place in 1710 than archives have recorded. Foundations of the present church cut through floors and levels of an earlier structure. Underneath everything, remnants of pottery were found. Indians had occupied the site, probably as early as 1300 A.D.

Around 1760 the Chapel of Our Lady of Light was built on the south side of the Plaza. Old documents and records state that this was "the handsomest building of its kind in the capital city." By the time Kearney's forces reached Santa Fe, it was in disuse and the roof had fallen in. Military authorities took over the building, removing all religious objects except the heavy, beautifully carved stone *reredos* (altar piece) which now graces the altar at Cristo Rey Church. Cristo Rey, located on Canyon Road, was built in 1939 and is one of the largest adobe buildings in the Americas.

In November of 1851, Father Jean Baptiste Lamy, a French priest in Ohio, was appointed Vicar Apostolic for Santa Fe, and in 1853 he became Santa Fe's first Bishop. He was appalled by the condition of the old adobe parish church, and he determined to build a new one in European style, to be named in honor of St. Francis. Lamy collected funds in Mexico and Europe. He imported Italian and French architects and stonemasons who taught natives how to quarry and cut the stone nearby in Arroyo Saiz and Lamy Junction. The stately naves rose above the older adobe church, where services continued as usual.

St. Francis Cathedral was built in the Mid-Romanesque style of Bishop Lamy's native Cleremont, France. The imported stained glass windows, the delicate stonework and the architectural lines themselves give the cathedral a distinctly European flavor. The style of the cathedral, and that of Loretto Chapel nearby on Old Santa Fe Trail, contrast dramatically with the smooth, rounded adobe of most of the rest of downtown Santa Fe. Today, St. Francis Cathedral continues to be the center of religious ceremonies during the annual Fiestas de Santa Fe, and serves the faithful throughout the year.

The Catholic Church in Santa Fe went through many phases: Colonization fervor, defeat before the antagonism of the native Indian peoples, reconstruction and embellishment, and finally a new, exalted status when New Mexico became an Archdiocese. Through their centuries of change, both the cathedral and San Miguel Chapel have retained enough of the old to mellow their appearance, yet give clues to old Santa Fe's less tranquil past.

Of special interest at St. Francis Cathedral is the chapel of *La Conquistadora*. Located at the north side of the cathedral and graced with a small wooden statue which many believe to be the country's oldest madonna, the chapel is the most ancient part of the cathedral. In 1625 Fray Alonso Benavides, Franciscan Superior of the New Mexico missions, brought the statue of Our Lady of the Assumption to Santa Fe's parish church. She was regarded not only as the Queen of Heaven but also *La Conquistadora*—the conqueror. Does her name refer to the fact that De Vargas brought her back during the Reconquest, or that she is the conquerer of men's souls?

On the triumphant reconquest of Santa Fe in 1693, General de Vargas and his men knelt in homage before *La Conquistadora* and vowed to honor her in a solemn procession. Today, in memory of this promise, *La Conquistadora* is carried each year from St. Francis Cathedral to Rosario Chapel, built in the early nineteenth century in the northwestern sector of town. She is enshrined there for nine days and then brought back to the Cathedral.

Very near St. Francis Cathedral is Loretto Chapel, one of the earliest Gothic church buildings west of the Mississippi. Archbishop Lamy requested its construction. Built between 1873 and 1878, Loretto is modelled after Sainte-Chapelle in Paris. Its lovely "miraculous" spiral staircase and the legend surrounding it are quite famous and charm every visitor.

Still another historic church is Our Lady of Guadalupe, a mission-style building which dates from the late 1700s. Situated picturesquely next to the Santa Fe River, Guadalupe Church once watched over the Denver & Rio Grande Railway's Chile Line as it rolled into town from the north every day. In 1961, to accommodate a growing parish, a new church was built alongside the old. The old church, popularly called the *Santuario de Guadalupe*, was remodelled in the 1970s and now serves as center for Hispanic art and cultural events, as well as musical activity.

THE NATIVE ART SCENE

Pueblo Indian pottery and weaving were flourishing in the Santa Fe area before the European discovery of the continent. The same symbols that decorate the pottery, weaving and jewelry of today are found on prehistoric items excavated by archaeologists. The Spanish introduced silverwork and the weaving of wool to the Indians, but the Pueblos were workers of turquoise and weavers of cotton and other fabrics long before Europeans arrived.

The best Indian jewelry is made entirely by hand. Today, one can find beautiful handmade jewelry being sold by Indians under the *portal* of the Palace of the Governors, as well as in the dozens of Indian arts shops in the city. Popular (and expensive) are the exquisite concha belts and "squash blossom" style necklaces.

The isolation of Spanish New Mexico in the 17th and 18th centuries forced people to be self-reliant. Many customs from 16th century Spain were carried well into the 19th century and a few are present even today. In remote mountain villages, nuances of New Mexican spoken Spanish trace back to 16th century Castillian Spanish. Uniquely New Mexico Spanish arts and crafts include carved *santos* (holy figures), furniture, chests, embroidered linens, woven serapes, tin frames and silver jewelry.

The finer things of life in Spanish colonial days were expressed in religion, folk music, drama and fiestas. Theatre was largely religious drama at Christmas and Easter. Early Franciscans painted on deer skin and buffalo hide to illustrate the Bible and the saints to the Pueblo Indians. Folk songs (which can still be heard in northern villages) enriched moments of relaxation.

Weavers spun sheep's wool and wove clothing, blankets and *yergas* (rugs). Yergas were woven in lengths about two feet wide, which were then sewn together to form wall-to-wall carpeting over earth floors. *Sabanilla*, a plain-weave homespun, was used for men's breeches, women's skirts and Franciscan habits. The colcha stitch was a unique expression in local tapestry. Exquisite examples of colcha, and other crafts are in the Museum of International Folk Art, which you will explore in the **St. John's/Lejo Walk.**

One of the most unique creations of New Mexico Spanish artistry is the *santo,* popular even to this day. There are two kinds: A carved wooden statue of a saint is called a *santo bulto;* an image of a saint painted on a small panel of wood is a *retablo.* The *santeros* were and still are largely farmers of the northern villages who carve to keep busy during the winter. The santo was treated as a family member. And it has been said that if prayers to the image went unanswered, it was turned to face the wall in disgrace.

Straw and corn husks were used for decorating hanging shelves that held family treasures. Today, there has been a renewed interest in Hispanic art with straw. Fine examples of this genre can be found, along with carvings and tinwork, at the Spanish Arts and Crafts Fair on the plaza in Santa Fe each summer.

In the 19th century, tin was known as the "silver of the poor". Brought by Yankee traders across the Santa Fe Trail in the form of tin containers, the material was cut up and shaped into candleholders, frames for mirrors and pictures, sconces, lanterns, boxes and trays. As with straw art, tinwork has enjoyed a renaissance among Spanish artisans, and many fine examples of this craft are being created today.

THE "ANGLO" ART SCENE

Santa Fe began to draw Anglo artists soon after New Mexico was occupied by the U.S. Army in 1846. By the early decades of the 20th century, a community of artists had formed that included important New York figures such as Robert Henri and John Sloan, and the legendary "Cinco Pintores".

These early painters were attracted by the brilliance of the sun, the clear air, and the intensity of color at 7,000 feet. The mountains and pinon-covered landscape were exotic to the eastern eye. The idea of the wild west captivated many early artists, and they strove to capture for immortality the "unspoiled" Indian on canvas.

Los Cinco Pintores (the five painters) banded together in 1921 to show their work as a group. The five were Will Schuster, Joseph Bakos, Willard Nash, Walter Mruk and Fremont Ellis. They lived and worked mainly along Camino del Monte Sol, a street which today is one of Santa Fe's loveliest and most pricey residential areas.

The Museum of Fine Arts was opened in 1917, and further helped establish the Santa Fe art environment. From this beginning, the number of private galleries in the city has grown to well over 100. They can be found surrounding the Plaza, tucked away on side streets, and lining Canyon Road. Santa Fe has become one of the top three art markets in America. It is claimed that Santa Fe has more original artwork for sale than any other American city except for New York and Los Angeles.

Another very strong influence on Santa Fe's art scene is the Institute of American Indian Arts. This government school for talented young Indian artists from all over the country has fostered such modern Indian painters as Fritz Scholder and T. C. Cannon. The Institute has an art museum open to the public.

Santa Fe has blossomed in many cultural directions. Surrounded by piñons, tall poplars, and not-so-distant mountains, Santa Fe Opera is now a mecca for connoisseurs. Established in 1957, SFO has become internationally famous. New Mexico Repertory Theatre, Greer Garson Theatre, and the historic Community Theatre are but a few of the city's acting companies. The city boasts two orchestras and the renowned Santa Fe Chamber Music Festival.

THE NEW FACE OF SANTA FE

A few years back Santa Fe experienced a sudden flurry of national publicity. Magazines such as *Esquire,* *The Rolling Stone, National Geographic* and *Rocky Mountain Magazine* have presented the city variously as a singles capital, an artists' haven, a retreat for the rich and famous, and a "living Old Town". For better or for worse, being "discovered" has resulted in a building and development boom for this ancient city.

Many old buildings in or near the downtown area have been converted into galleries, luxury condominiums and offices. There are an amazing number of doctors and lawyers per capita. One by one, the older stores downtown are moving out to shopping centers. In their stead are luxury clothing stores, gift and specialty shops, restaurants and more galleries.

Old-timers complain that their city is becoming too touristy, over-commercialized, crowded and expensive. But perhaps these changes were simply inevitable. Desirable locations—places with quality environments and pleasurable lifestyles—will naturally attract sizeable influxes of people from "somewhere else". But if I'd moved to Santa Fe in the eighties rather than the sixties, I would still want to stay.

Your excursions on foot will no doubt reveal to you more and more of Santa Fe's special, enduring appeal.

I. THE PLEASURES OF WALKING

Museum of Fine Arts

Walking is humankind's most ancient form of exercise, and most fitness authorities feel that it is the best. As soon as they stood upright, people began covering vast territories on foot. Walking enjoyed great popularity during the Romantic Age in England, when poets such as Wordsworth took lengthy, extended walks to fuel the imagination and to store visual pictures for their poetry. In our country, walking has been rediscovered as a very beneficial conditioner. It is similar to running and swimming in that it involves continual movement. In other words, it is "aerobic", and if done with reasonable vigor will push lungs, heart and muscles to utilize oxygen more effectively.

Walking is no longer in the shade of the "running boom", but during the last decade has come into its own. And there are quite a few advantages. First, it is an activity for every age, including children and older people. It requires no special training, except perhaps building up stamina for longer distances. It has the advantage of allowing you to carry more than if you were running. A daypack or rucksack can be packed with books, binoculars, camera, sketchpad or notebook, food and drink. And an occasional extra item or two of clothing. The larger "fanny packs" can do the same, and free your shoulders of any burden.

Walking is conducive to browsing—looking into museums, libraries, galleries and shops. That is why the first routes section of this book, which include the downtown area and Santa Fe's major museums, is devoted to routes for walking. However, any area that can be walked can also be run.

Just a word here about maps. In charting your "on foot" excursions of Santa Fe, you'll no doubt want to use a larger overall map of the city, as well as those included in the book. There are city maps for sale throughout Santa Fe, at service stations, book stores, and even grocery stores. The Horton Family book, *Street Maps,* is an excellent guide. The Santa Fe Chamber of Commerce gives out a free Street Guide. And of course, there's always the map provided at the end of the Santa Fe phone directory.

Though walking is beautifully simple, there are a few things which should be kept in mind to get the most from the experience. It cannot be stressed too often that Santa Fe's weather changes rapidly. We have a mountain climate, and though there is abundant sunshine, a day's weather can alter radically within an hour. In summer and fall, you should always carry a rain poncho (no matter how clear the morning looks); in winter and into spring, snowstorms and flurries often happen without much announcement except for a few gathering clouds. We're at high altitude where the sun's rays are strong and relatively unfiltered, so be particularly aware of the need for a hat and sunglasses. Keep everything together in a light pack, and you'll always be prepared to hit the road.

Walking is considered safer than running or bicycling. You are able to respond to changes in terrain or traffic with more agility. But watch your footing and try not to get so transported by Santa Fe's natural beauty that you miss potholes or roadside obstacles. There are few, if any, rattlesnakes in town, though there are many dogs on the loose. I have found that a raised stick or tossed pebbles will ward off even the fiercest barkers. It's best to avoid trying to make friends. Let dogs know that you see them, keep a watchful eye as you pass, and if you're moved to throw rocks, try just to intimidate rather than actually pelt them. A friend says every mean dog knows what a rock in a raised hand means, and nearly all will back off without a shot being fired. Santa Fe has a "leash law" but it is rarely enforced. If an area turns out to be just too "doggy", take a detour and then continue your planned route.

If you're from out of town, be sure to allow for the effects of altitude—shortness of breath, less energy and lightheadedness—when you first arrive. Take the shorter walks at first, then graduate to lengthier ones.

However you go about it, and whatever your chosen mode or mood, walking is the best way to get back on your own two feet!

PLAZA AREA/
CANYON ROAD/
OLD SANTA FE TRAIL
WALK

So, you've decided to walk and/or run Santa Fe! You'll be in for some of the most beautiful views of mountains, cityscape and high desert to be found anywhere. You'll see a lot of variety in the supposedly uniform adobe architecture. You will breathe, smell and feel Santa Fe in a way that those behind the wheel never can. And with today's five-mile tour, you'll also absorb a lot of local history in the bargain.

The nearly 400 years of Santa Fe's written history, not to mention the untold chronicles of the pueblo which occupied Santa Fe's site for centuries before, come to light as one walks around the Plaza and through the museums which are included in both this Walk and the next. However, do not expect a history disguised as a walking and running book. If you want to learn more, visit the city, state and museum libraries, as well as the New Mexico Records Center and Archives. Collections at these institutions, all of which are open to the public, offer in-depth reading on every aspect of Santa Fe's past and present.

Any tour of Santa Fe must begin with the Plaza and adjacent areas. The Plaza, despite recent talk about the new "center" of town being out on St. Michael's Drive, is still the heart of the city. If no longer true in the usual commercial sense, the Plaza remains culturally, spiritually and artistically the center of things. It was from this heart that the

Canyon Road, Santa Fe's arts and crafts road.

arteries of early Santa Fe led. East Palace Avenue was (and still is) lined with elegant mansions belonging to its most prominent and prosperous citizens. The academic centers of the mid-1800s, St. Michael's College and the Loretto Academy, were located a few steps from the plaza on Old Santa Fe Trail. It was at the Plaza, of course, where Don Diego de Peralta, third governor of New Mexico, established the official capital in 1610. And it is here that the oldest continuously occupied governmental building in the country, the Palace of the Governors, stands so venerably.

All subsequent development of Santa Fe, after the establishment of the Palace of the Governors, was built around and then grew out from the Plaza. Though a few of their names may have changed, the original roads and trails which radiated outward from the city's nucleus are still in use today.

Except for one hilly portion, today's walk is moderate. It is mostly unshaded, however. Your equipment should include a protective hat and/or sunglasses. As with any Santa Fe walk or run, you're well advised to wear sunscreen, depending on the vulnerability of your skin. A small canteen may make the walk more pleasant on warm days. Santa Fe is known for abrupt changes in weather: take a windbreaker or poncho.

Year-round, Santa Fe usually reaches its warmest between 11:00 a.m. and 3:00 p.m. Because of this, I prefer saving an inside look at the Palace of the Governors and the Fine Arts Museum until the end of the hike. The walking itself, at a moderate pace, should take only a couple of hours. If you allow half an hour for a picnic lunch and an hour for each museum, you will need four or five hours all told.

Be a bit leisurely at the start. The Plaza, with its white wrought iron park benches, brick walkways and canopy of American elms, cottonwoods, green ash, honey locust, firs and maples, has an atmosphere of comfort and civility. Like the businesses on three sides, the Plaza has changed and evolved throughout the centuries. Before the beginning of Victorian influences in the 1800s it was all dirt—dusty in summer, muddy during winter. Some early photographs show it ringed by trees and circled by an *acequia* (irrigation ditch).

According to Ralph E. Twitchell's *Old Santa Fe* (1925), the Plaza was laid out according to Spanish ordinances of the 1500s. The center of the city was always to be rectangular rather than square, "at least one and a half times as long as it was wide," in order to allow room for the horses which were always part of military and religious processions. Sometime throughout the course of events, however, the Plaza became shortened. It once included the business block on the east

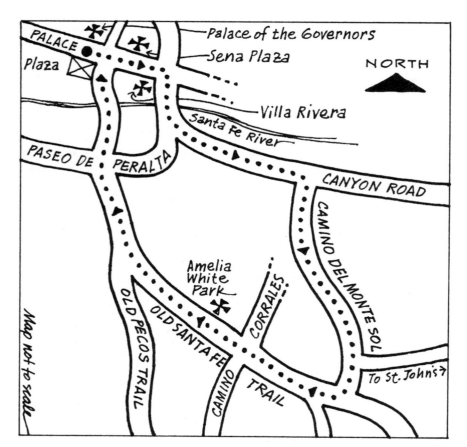

Palace of the Governors

Sena Plaza

NORTH

PALACE

Plaza

Villa Rivera

Santa Fe River

PASEO DE PERALTA

CANYON ROAD

CAMINO DEL MONTE SOL

Amelia White Park

CORRALES

OLD PECOS TRAIL

OLD SANTA FE TRAIL

CAMINO

To St. John's →

Map not to scale

side, and thus extended to the cathedral site. From time to time, Santa Fe city officials block traffic from the Plaza. Usually, however, traffic travels around it in a counterclockwise direction. Exercise caution during the summer; though cars are moving slowly, drivers tend to be sightseeing rather than paying attention to pedestrians.

Think back now to the 1600s. The space where you are standing was the scene of daily markets, cockfights, public floggings and social gatherings. All around were the low-lying city's houses and farms. To the north, as it does today, loomed the Palace of the Governors. Later, during Territorial times, the city's nucleus was the scene of trading, dance halls and gambling dens. Today the Plaza is still used for concerts, fiesta, downtown fairs such as the Indian and Spanish Markets, and community events of all kinds.

In the center of the Plaza stands a stone obelisk. Created in 1868, it is dedicated to "the heroes of the Federal Army who fell at the Battle of Valverde... (and) who fell at the battles of Canon del Apache and Pigeon's Ranch (La Glorieta)." The east side of the obelisk proclaims "May the Union be Perpetual." New Mexico was allied with Union forces during the Civil War.

In the southwest quadrant of the Plaza is a granite marker commemorating the end of the Santa Fe Trail.

After caravans of goods arrived, their cargo was unloaded, traded and stored in local warehouses. Goods came from Colorado, Kansas and Missouri, as well as from Chihuahua, Mexico. In early 1880, when the transcontinental railroad reached Santa Fe, the commercial importance of the Santa Fe Trail diminished. The city strengthened its connections with the modern world of railroad commerce.

Today, at the northeast end of the Plaza, you will see the large pink Catron Building. Its arched windows, elaborate ornamental brackets and angularity identify it as part of Santa Fe's Victorian era. Now the Catron Building houses offices and clothing stores, uses that it has had since 1912. Before leaving the Plaza, you might want to take a drink, or fill your canteen, from the water fountain at the northwest corner.

Stroll along in front of the Palace and enjoy the Pueblo Indians' open air market. As long as anyone can remember, the Indians have been selling their pottery and jewelry here. At the east end of the Palace *portal*, pause to read the plaque marking the site of Santa Fe's first chapel, which apparently doubled as a defense tower during the 1600s. Cross Washington Avenue, staying on the left, and you'll find yourself at Prince and Sena Plazas, two ancient adobe structures that are now a series of shops.

The land that Sena Plaza now occupies was part of

the property of Captain Arias de Quiros, which eventually came into the ownership of Major Juan Sena. This gentleman and his wife, Dona Isabel Cabeza de Baca, had 23 children. The Sena home was expanded into a 33-room enclosed fortress. Everything except the ballroom was on ground level. In the 1890s, after the capitol of the territory burned, the ballroom served as temporary legislative meeting place.

It was primarily Miss Amelia White, a philanthropist who moved to Santa Fe from New York in 1923, who took the initiative in preserving Sena Plaza. She and her sister Martha took great pains to make the restoration authentic, yet the addition of a second story all around was Amelia's project. This lady, a music lover and generous humanitarian, did much for the city of Santa Fe. (According to Charlotte White, her companion from 1942 until her death, "Never was there a woman who did so much and was forgotten so fast.")

Pause to look inside Sena Plaza's courtyard. Remaining true to its original purpose, it is a restful haven, geometrically laid out and graced with trees and flowers. At the northwest courtyard corner was the household's larder and cooking area, now a popular Southwestern style restaurant. In the warmer months, the courtyard is filled with nasturtiums, roses, hollyhocks, geraniums, petunias, mums, sweet-peas, holly and juniper. A fountain and benches have been added.

Walk east along Palace Avenue's brick sidewalk and peruse the plaques along the walls. Reads one: "In 1879 bought by L. Bradford Prince (later Territorial Governor)." States another: "In 1942 bought by Field Estate for Enlisted Men's Club in World War II."

About 3/10ths of a mile from the start, at the stoplight, you will be turning right on Paseo de Peralta. On the southwest corner of Palace and Peralta stand two painted brick buildings that represent an important force in shaping Santa Fe's past. They are an older and newer portion of the complex that used to be St. Vincent Hospital. The older building, Marian Hall, was built in 1865 by the Catholic Church and the Sisters of Charity to house the hospital. The Sisters very competently ran what for years was the only hospital in the southwest. After the newer structure on the corner was built, members of the order who were sent to serve in Santa Fe continued to reside in Marian Hall. Now a public building, the hall once included a very handsome chapel with lovely stained glass windows.

In addition to the hospital and Marian Hall, the Sisters of Charity also ran an orphanage. Operating from 1890 until 1950, it was the only one of its kind west of the Mississippi. The hospital eventually moved to southeastern Santa Fe, and the huge corner property was acquired by the state. What used to be the hospital has been renamed Villa Rivera, after a well-loved priest who was murdered a few years ago. It houses state offices as well as La Residencia nursing home.

Also on this corner, across Palace Avenue from Villa Rivera, is the Willi Spiegelberg house. This attractive yellow and white building dates from the mid 1800s. It was built by a prominent merchant, who with his four brothers ran one of the most successful mercantile stores of the time.

On still another corner, across Peralta from Villa Rivera, is another bit of Santa Fe's history. Nestled amid lush grounds and large old trees is La Posada de Santa Fe. Now an inn, the main part of this complex of buildings was an ornate mansion belonging to pioneer Santa Fe businessman and merchant Abraham Staab. Begun in 1882, the Staab home took four years to complete. In 1934, the mansion was converted to a hotel. The Staab House, still decorated in the original Victorian mode, was the scene of countless social extravaganzas and is today a fashionable lounge and meeting place. The ghost of Mrs. Julie Staab is said by some to sob and roam disconsolately around the second floor.

Take a right at the corner and proceed south on busy Paseo de Peralta. Look to your left as you stroll and you'll be rewarded with glimpses of the lovely *Sangre de Cristo* mountains, translated "Blood of Christ". Some claim the mountains were named for the sunset's glow on the snow-capped peaks. This is just one of several mountainscapes on this route.

Continue south on Peralta. When you come to Alameda Street you'll cross a bridge over the Santa Fe River. Despite the fact that the river usually runs at very low ebb, proof of its influence is the fertile strip along either side: abundant grass and towering old cottonwoods. The river park is cherished as a walkers' haven. In mild weather, many people who work in the city's businesses and shops bring picnic lunches to enjoy at one of the riverside tables. Year-round, runners can be seen on this narrow park's dirt paths.

After crossing the river, look for the beginning of Canyon Road on your left. It's well-marked with a sign announcing "The Arts and Crafts Road." As you walk up Canyon Road, you enter what was during the early 1900s one of Santa Fe's main thoroughfares. In the twenties, Canyon Road first acquired its artistic character. The famous *"Los Cinco Pintores"* (five painters who moved here from the east) banded together in this neighborhood to paint and promote their work. As you walk uphill you'll pass abundant reminders of their influence.

Narrow and irregular, this charming road offers a few challenges to the walker. The sidewalk along the left side at times dwindles to a tiny path. During summer, cars may be bumper to bumper. In other words, exercise a healthy caution as you enjoy Canyon Road's ambience.

There's a lot here: antique shops, framers, art suppliers, restaurants, clothing boutiques, and stores specializing in gold and silver jewelry, leather, stained glass, or crystal. There are clusters of private homes and, of course, art galleries and artists' studios. Within the first block, a short driveway on the left leads to Project Tibet, an organization that helps Tibetan refugees in Nepal, India, and Bhutan, and also markets Tibetan handicrafts.

Across from Project Tibet on a hillock stands the red brick First Ward Schoolhouse, now a gallery. Further along you'll encounter El Zaguan (a *zaguan* is a long covered passageway or corridor), a rambling hacienda which has served as a home, a general store, a private girls' school and now rental apartments. Along the street side of this remarkable building is a lime green picket fence. Right before the fence you'll be able to look into the gardens planted by pioneer archaeologist Adolph Bandelier. El Zaguan dates from the 1700s and a part of it now serves as headquarters for the Historic Santa Fe Foundation.

In the block after El Zaguan, on the opposite side of the road, you'll find the tiny Olive Rush Studio, a beautifully preserved adobe which was used by that artist during the early 1900s. Miss Rush was a devoted Quaker, and the building has been used most recently as the meeting house for Santa Fe's Society of Friends.

Meander further up Canyon Road. Near the corner of Canyon and Camino del Monte Sol, you'll encounter the historic Borrego House, a rambling, territorial style building that dates from 1839. For the past few decades, this site has housed various restaurants. Clustered at this juncture of roads are several other popular restaurants and watering spots.

When you reach Camino del Monte Sol, turn right off Canyon onto "The Camino". This mile-long road includes some of Santa Fe's loveliest homes and gardens. There are large trees along the way, and you can look forward to partial shade. You'll find dusty-green Russian olive trees, junipers, spruce, firs and ponderosa pine, tall poplars, feathery tamarisk. There are also typical Santa Fe plants such as *cholla* cacti, the ubiquitous *chamisa*, lilacs, yellow and orange roses of Castile, and Virginia creeper. Take time to glance left for a prospect of the Sangre de Cristos and foothills. Enjoy the adobe walls, with their soft contours and niches, as well as the juniper pole "coyote fences" (perhaps named for the varmints they were originally intended to keep out). As you climb this enchanting stretch, be on the lookout for cars at all times. The route is narrow and shoulderless.

As you continue south, the landscape begins to open up. After passing the turnoff to Santa Fe Preparatory School and St. John's College, you will reach the end of Camino del Monte Sol. Here you can look forward to two final miles of downhill and flat terrain. Take a right-hand turn on Old Santa Fe Trail and then cross to the left-hand side of the road. There is a dirt path right above the curb. Better to take this than to stay next to the fast-moving traffic.

You may want to take note of the road on your left (Camino Lejo) that leads to a complex of museums. You will explore these on the **St. John's/Lejo Museums Walk** in this book.

This is a relaxing downhill stretch where you can breathe deeply and enjoy two of Santa Fe's most salutory assets: Fresh, invigorating air and serene mountain vistas. Right along this particular stretch of Santa Fe Trail you'll be able to take in three of the city's mountainscapes. To your left (southwest) the distant Sandias near Albuquerque; to your right (northwest) the massive and volcanic Jemez; and to your right and back, the Sangre de Cristos. The Sangres and the Jemez are often snow-capped by October. They'll remain so until the beginning of summer. The sharp contrast between snow and brilliant sunshine can be exhilirating; it is a landscape I often feel like drinking in. In feeling at least, this is a good stretch on which to meditate and reflect in country-like atmosphere.

At the Camino Corrales intersection, which you'll be coming to shortly, is a particularly spectacular view of the Sangres to the right. Ahead, you'll be able to take in an excellent view of the sunbaked, pinon-dotted hills of north Santa Fe.

When you reach Corrales, you might take a slight detour to the quiet Amelia White Park at this intersection. It was originally intended by Miss White to be a memorial for soldiers who had died in Korea. There remains a formal gravelled square with eight planters of roses and lilacs, as well as a monument to the war veterans and a defunct fountain. Local journalists have referred to this spot as "Forgotten Park", a comment on its neglect as well as its remarkable serenity. The city has recently added a long, covered arbor and a wooden fence along the border. It's a good spot to relax on a bench and perhaps enjoy any snacks you might have packed along.

After your respite, continue down Old Santa Fe Trail. The path you'd followed before is now erratic, sometimes on the left, sometimes on the right. It's best after leaving the park to stay on the left facing traffic until you approach the 'Y' intersection with

Old Pecos Trail, then cross to the right side.

At the Y, continue downhill along Old Santa Fe Trail into the more "urban" scene of this historic old entryway to the Plaza area. I recommend taking the right-hand sidewalk.

The last mile of your walk is packed with interesting sights. You'll see small adobe homes, a boot repair shop, a barber shop, a religious artifacts emporium, antique and carpet shops, restaurants. When you come to Santa Fe Trail's intersection with Paseo de Peralta, you'll see the massive "Round House", New Mexico's capitol building, to your left. Take time to walk around its attractive landscaped grounds.

Further down the Trail on your right you'll pass San Miguel Chapel, the oldest church in America and the nearby alleged "Oldest House" (it was part of the Pueblo village that predated the city). Cross the Alameda and continue toward the heart of the City on Old Santa Fe Trail. On your right, just past the Inn at Loretto, stands the graceful Loretto Chapel. This Chapel, with its Gothic interior and "miraculous staircase", was built in the 1870s by the Sisters of Loretto. Admission is 25 cents—hearing the charming tale of the staircase is well worth the price.

You'll make a slight jog left and then right where Old Santa Fe Trail intersects with Water Street. A block later you'll reach the Plaza. Along the north side of the last block of Old Santa Fe Trail is the towering (five story) La Fonda, long the main hostelry in the heart of Santa Fe. This was the site of the Exchange Hotel, which greeted the famous and infamous at the end of the long, dusty ride west from Independence, Missouri, or north from Chihuahua, Mexico.

If you didn't do so at the beginning of the day, take time now to visit the Palace of the Governors. Built in 1610, this edifice served as crown and military capitol of Spain's northern empire in the New World. Both governmental seat and fortress in the early days, it is now the only surviving part of a much larger complex of *Casas Reales*. The adobe Palace was the seat of power for Spanish, Pueblo Revolt and Mexican reigns, as well as U.S. Territorial Capitol from 1846 until the end of the century. It was held for a few days by Confederate forces. Today it is part of the state museum. The Palace's artifacts, photographs and exhibits provide vivid illustrations of New Mexico's history.

Just west of the Palace of the Governors stands the Museum of Fine Arts. End your tour with a visit to this outstanding Pueblo-style edifice and its wide-ranging collection of Southwestern paintings, photographs, sculptures and drawings. The building, which was modelled after Acoma Pueblo's church and other New Mexico mission buildings, is a fine work of art in itself. St. Francis Auditorium, an acoustically excellent theatre, is the home of many of the city's fine musical events.

The Palace of the Governors and the Museum of Fine Arts are open daily from 10:00 a.m. to 5:00 p.m., except in January and February when they're closed on Mondays. Docents conduct daily tours, and tours can be arranged by appointment the year round. Admission is $3.00 for adults and $1.25 for children (6-16 years). A two-day pass good at all four state museums is $5.00 for adults and $2.50 for children. On Sunday, admission for New Mexico residents is $1.00. The telephone number for general information is (505) 827-6463.

Immaculate Heart of Mary Seminary, as seen from Old Santa Fe Trail.

ST. JOHN'S COLLEGE / LEJO MUSEUMS WALK

Today's route, nestled close to the Sangre de Cristo foothills on the southeastern edge of the city, is one of my favorites. It takes the hiker from one of Santa Fe's three colleges, St. John's, past Santa Fe Preparatory School, around a monastery circa the 1940s, and through four museums. Except for the first section, with its moderate but rather long slope, the route is relatively flat. Total distance is 5½ miles. The terrain, as with many of these walks, is well suited for bicycling and running as well as walking.

Begin your tour at St. John's College, located near the end of Camino de la Cruz Blanca. (This short road takes off near the top end of Camino del Monte Sol.) If you've driven here, park your car at the college complex in the area marked "Visitors".

Before embarking on the walk itself, take time out to stroll around the campus. St. John's College at Santa Fe was established in 1964. One of the oldest schools in the country, the parent institution in Annapolis dates back to 1696. Both schools offer a four-year program based on the great books of the western world. Learning takes place through seminars and "tutorials". The professors (or tutors, as they're referred to here) act more as advanced students than traditional lecturers.

The St. John's philosophy maintains that the way to liberal education lies through the works in which

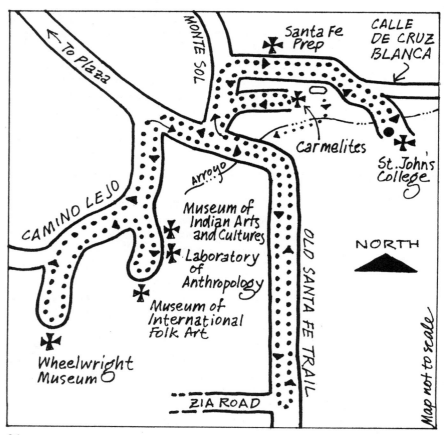

MONTE SOL

← To Plaza

Santa Fe Prep

CALLE DE CRUZ BLANCA

Carmelites

St. John's College

CAMINO LEJO

Arroyo

Museum of Indian Arts and Cultures

Laboratory of Anthropology

Museum of International Folk Art

Wheelwright Museum

NORTH

OLD SANTA FE TRAIL

ZIA ROAD

Map not to scale

the greatest minds of our civilization have expressed themselves. The original thinkers serve as guides: students learn math from studying Euclid, physics from Einstein and psychology from Freud, and so forth. St. John's in Santa Fe maintains a rapidly growing Graduate Institute, offering a master of arts in liberal education. Full-time enrollment at the college hovers at about 300. Many Santa Feans avail themselves of the college's community seminar program.

The campus consists of territorial style buildings attractively trimmed in white, situated dramatically at the foot of Sun Mountain. Its dormitories and classrooms are tiered down the pinon-covered hillside. Peterson Student Center, located mid-campus, has a coffee shop, water fountains and restrooms, as well as an art gallery and library. The college sponsors films, lectures, and concerts open to the public.

After your look about, head back down the broad, meandering driveway to Camino de la Cruz Blanca. Not surprisingly, the air at St. John's seems even clearer and fresher than in the city's center (the campus is about 300 feet higher). Breathe in deeply and feast your eyes on the 360 degree view: the Sangre de Cristo foothills to your right, the Sandias and Ortiz mountains to the left, and ahead the Jemez range.

There are two ways to reach the Carmelite Monastery, the next highlight of your walk. The first (which I'll call *Route 1*) takes you downhill through the arroyo and leads to a turnstile opening up to Old Santa Fe Trail. The second (*Route 2*) is simply walking down Camino de la Cruz Blanca and taking left turns till you come to the monastery. Each has advantages. You can read about them now and take your pick.

Decided to climb down into the arroyo? For *Route 1*, follow the college driveway all the way out, take a left on Camino Cruz Blanca, pass the tennis courts and a grassy field, and walk all the way to the end of the cinder track. Go downhill through a light pinon forest till you reach the arroyo itself. You may have to zigzag, as there is no direct path. It's an easy walk through the arroyo's sandy bottom, and a completely different environment. You'll see up close a remarkable array of wild desert plants and wildflowers in season—plus an occasional jackrabbit, harmless stink beetle, lizard, or pinon jay. Soon you'll notice the arroyo passes under a bridge; here's where you veer to the left side of the arroyo and pass through a wooden turnstile that will take you up to the road— Old Santa Fe Trail. Keeping an eye out for the occasional speeder, turn right onto Old Santa Fe Trail, and walk to Camino del Monte Sol. Take a right here and walk another few hundred yards to Mount Carmel Road.

Going back to the St. John's track, here is what

you'll find if you choose to take *Route 2,* the road rather than the arroyo route: a gentle downhill slope on asphalt with a clear view of the mountains. There is no sidewalk, but there is a small path on the left, which I'd advise using. Going about Santa Fe on foot, you'll soon use the Sangre de Cristos, the Jemez and the Sandias as your landmarks. Their outlines are nearly always partially visible. Because of Santa Fe's endlessly varying skies, the mountains seem to change color and mood daily. The layers of blue, brown and green are sometimes smoked with a light haze; at other times they are as clearly defined as a construction paper collage. When the sky is overcast with winter, the mountains often glow with streaks of sunlight. Luminously bigger than life; sometimes brown, sometimes blue, purple or green; often snow-mantled: the mountains bordering Santa Fe have a magic about them that soothes and inspires. As you run and walk the city, seeing the mountainscapes from different angles and in different weather, you may find it hard to believe that you are looking at the same scene. In a way, you aren't.

On the right-hand side of Cruz Blanca, after you've passed the St. John's track, you'll see the campus of Santa Fe Preparatory School. Established in 1964 by parents who saw the need for a private, non-denominational day school in Santa Fe, Prep moved from its original Upper Canyon Road location to Cruz Blanca in 1971. Offering college-oriented education to children from grades seven through twelve, Prep has established a firm local reputation. The field just beyond the campus complex and adjacent to the road is used for soccer, lacrosse and field hockey.

When you reach Camino del Monte Sol, take a left, walk just a tenth of a mile and then turn left again at Mount Carmel Road. This is the entrance to the Sacred Heart of Mary Seminary. As you walk up the long drive, you'll be facing a church. The Pueblo-style chapel, attended mainly by the seminarians and the Carmelite nuns, is fronted with mosaic religious scenes done by some local artists. On your right, after you first enter the grounds, is the convent occupied by the Carmelites. Beyond this complex are classrooms, a gym, a large administration building and dormitories for the seminarians.

The monastery, established in 1947, is the most recent chapter in the history of a piece of land which has seen many uses, including a sanitarium, a tent city, and a luxury hotel. As you amble about the present-day religious complex, you may find it interesting to speculate on the site's past.

During the 1880s, tuberculosis in the country accelerated to epidemic proportions. Throughout California, Texas, Colorado and New Mexico, sanitariums flourished. Along with the romance of going West, the quest for good health also brought visitors to Santa Fe. It was fashionable for eastern doctors back then to send their patients out West for cures. There was great debate, in fact, over which "sans" had the best air, wind and sunshine. A new medical specialty developed, one relating to variations in weather, temperature and altitude as they bore upon curing TB. In a keen race for the health seekers' dollars, entrepreneurs busily transformed existing hotels into sanitariums.

In a 1903 issue, the *Santa Fe New Mexican* addressed the problem of accomodations for tourists and announced Sunmount Tent City, a suburb intended to accommodate tourists, transient visitors and health seekers. The village at Sunmount, modelled after a famous tent city in Coronado, California, was to eventually include wide avenues, ample gardens, a sewage system and a casino. The tents, which were rented by the city for ten or fifteen dollars a month, were supposed to be habitable in temperatures below zero. Whether it was because the tents were impractical or the master plan never was completed, Sunmount was not particularly successful.

In 1920, Sunmount Company of Santa Fe became an official sanitarium and operated in conjunction with the tent city. By 1938, the sanitarium had been converted into a luxury hotel, Santa Fe Inn. The hotel and site changed hands in 1946, when the Archdiocese of Santa Fe purchased it as a monastery and seminary location. What had been the hotel became an administration building/dining hall. Gradually the chapel, dormitories, a gymnasium and classroom buildings were added.

When the institution was first established, it was a "minor seminary" for male high school freshmen up to college sophomores. In 1968, younger students were no longer admitted and the seminary became a four-year college program. Today, some 40 seminarians take their religious training at the seminary and their academic courses at the College of Santa Fe. They are involved in various ministries throughout the city—working with people at the jail and in nursing homes, as well as with deaf and otherwise handicapped. They also teach religion and physical education in some of the city's parochial schools. The seminary staff consists of six teachers. Although the institution is comparatively small, folks there are not opposed to occasional quiet visitors.

After your exploration of the seminary/monastery, walk back down Mt. Carmel Road and take a left where it runs into Camino del Monte Sol. In just a few yards, you will be at the Old Santa Fe Trail, where you turn right. The road slopes downhill and passes

Camino Lejo, the location of a remarkable complex of museums. When you reach Camino Lejo, you will have walked 1-⅓ miles.

Take a left and start along the asphalt road toward the museums. The road, which passes the official residence of the School of American Research's director, is bordered by some of the finest pinon trees in the area. They offer a touch of coolness in what has been so far a relatively unshaded walk. The first major turnoff from Lejo, 2/10ths of a mile from Santa Fe Trail, is for the Museum of Indian Arts and Cultures, Laboratory of Anthropology and the Museum of International Folk Art. The second turnoff, reached after Lejo has become a dirt road, leads to the Wheelwright Museum of the American Indian. All the museums are on the left (east) side of Camino Lejo.

The first museum structure you come to is the brand new Museum of Indian Arts and Cultures. A unit of the Museum of New Mexico, it was just being built as this edition of *Santa Fe On Foot* went to press. Call the Museum of New Mexico's information number, 827-6450, for information on exhibits and hours.

The oldest institution you will come to is the Laboratory of Anthropology, a lovely Spanish pueblo style building designed by John Gaw Meem, the dean of New Mexico architecture. It's right next door to the Indian Arts museum. Part of John D. Rockefeller's dream of founding a Southwestern anthropological center, the Laboratory of Anthropology was opened in 1931 for the purpose of research, education and publication. Amelia White and her sister donated most of the land, and Rockefeller supplied the initial funds. The New York philanthropist also pledged money for the Laboratory's first five years. It was assumed that at the end of that period, the lab would be self-sustaining. No one could forsee the severity or length of the upcoming depression which would bring to a halt the grand plan. World War II did even more to inhibit the Laboratory's development. The only buildings completed were the administration/ research building and auditorium (which now houses the Laboratory collection and library) and a residence (which is now owned by the School for American Research, a private archaeological research institution).

Even though the dreams of 1931 faded during the depression years, the Laboratory survived and is now a part of the state museum system. At one point during the 1940s the Lab was directed by Maurice Ries, a former newsman from Louisiana. Ries apparently felt that public relations were needed, and broadcast a radio program from the Anthropology Laboratory. In 1947, the Lab became a unit of the Museum of New Mexico. The staff is involved in a massive computerization of the 30,000-plus archeological sites in New

Mexico. The office of the State Archaeologist is also located here.

Two features of the Lab which are accessible primarily to scholars but can be viewed upon request by discreet visitors are the library, one of the most complete storehouses of anthropolological sources in the Southwest, and the superlative basement collection of pottery, weavings, rugs and other artifacts.

The Museum of International Folk Art shares a parking area with the Lab and the Indian Arts Museum. Proceed directly south to the long, angular building which houses one of the world's most unique and extensive collections of folk art. Established in 1953 as the result of efforts by humanitarian and folk art authority Florence Dibell Bartlett, this museum's collections are from all over the world. They include a stunning variety of costumes, Navajo pictorial weavings, Swedish folk art, New Mexican carved santos, Afro-Arabian items, toys from the Carribbean, musical instruments from the Indian subcontinent, and much more. The exhibits you'll see are a mere fraction of the total collections.

The Girard Wing of the Museum of International Folk Art opened in 1982. Drawn from the Alexander Girard Foundation Collection of over 100,000 folk art items, "Multiple Visions: A Common Bond", presents 10,000 items representing 100 different countries. The Mexican folk art collection, the work of Mrs. Girard, is said by many to be the finest in the world. The brilliant, witty juxtaposition of similar folk art from varying cultures is a delight. You will no doubt want to spend the rest of the day here. Resist the temptation, if you can, and save a thorough visit for another occasion. Like other units of the Museum of New Mexico, the Museum of International Folk Art is open Tuesday through Sunday from 9 a.m. till 5:00 p.m. During the summer season, March through October, it is also open on Monday. Call the Museum, 827-8350, for exhibit changes and any time changes.

Walk out of the Museum lot back to Camino Lejo, which becomes a dirt road beyond this first complex. You'll go down a dip, around a curve and uphill once more to approach the final musuem on this route. The Wheelwright Museum of the American Indian, founded in 1937, was originally known as The House of Navajo Religion, and subsequently the Museum of Navajo Ceremonial Art. Its origin was an outgrowth of the friendship of Mary Cabot Wheelwright and the esteemed Navajo medicine man, Hosteen Klah. Designed by Santa Fe artist William P. Henderson, the museum was built in the shape and spirit of a Navajo hogan. The collection of Klah's sacred medicine bundles has been transferred to Navajo Community College at the tribe's request, but the museum has retained

17 of the Klah family's sandpainting weavings.

Before entering the museum, partake of the grounds. The patio outside the entrance commands a particularly glorious view of the Sangre de Cristos. It's also the roof of the larger, below grade portion of the building. Note the modern totem pole, "Horse Fetish Totem #1"; the massive "Seated Woman" sculpture by R. C. Gorman; and the Allan Houser sculptures "Offering the Sacred Pipe" and "Heading Home".

The Case Trading Post, located in the museum's lower gallery, replicates a turn-of-the-century Navajo Reservation trading post. Almost everything is for sale here—weavings, pottery, basketry, contemporary paintings and sculpture, as well as posters, cards and books.

Museum hours are 10 a.m. till 5 p.m. Monday through Saturday, and from 1 till 5 p.m. on Sundays. From November through April, the museum is closed on Monday. Call 982-4636 for updates.

During the summer months, the Folk Art Museum has a small outdoor cafe open to the public. Fare is simple—sandwiches and local specialties—but quite good. You may wish to eat there, or you may rather enjoy your own picnic somewhere around the scenic Wheelwright grounds.

After lunch, you'll be ready for the last leg of today's excursion. Go back to Camino Lejo, retrace your steps back to the intersection with Old Santa Fe Trail, and turn right (east). Half a mile, more or less, beyond the Lejo turnoff, the Trail curves south and you'll come to the bridge that crosses over Arroyo Chamiso—the same arroyo that you viewed from St. John's College. (Or, the same arroyo you walked through to this point earlier, if you were adventuresome.)

The view from the bridge is worth a pause. You can see the window-filled south side of the former sanitarium turned monastery, the Santa Fe Ski Basin in the distance, and in the foreground the sandy, water-carved arroyo, an environment unto itself.

This viewpoint is also perfect for studying the Sangre de Cristo foothills. Archetypally New Mexican, they offer a montage of clay, rock outcroppings and pinons, in soft forms set against the dazzling sky. Monte Sol, or "Sun Mountain" as it is more frequently referred to, is closest to the seminary. A second hillock, similar in shape but a little smaller, abuts Sun Mountain. Not surprisingly, it is "Moon Mountain".

The shadings and contours of "mountains" such as Sun and Moon have inspired many an artist and sketcher. In nice weather it is not unusual to see an artist painting right at this bridge. The distant view of the ski basin area to the northeast serves as a harbinger of the changing seasons. Its predominate colors vary from purple to tan, brown or green—

browner in spring and fall, and green in spring and summer. When the aspen leaves turn gold and orange in the fall, the area is stunning both up close and from afar. From October till June, it wears a mantle of snow. During winter sunsets, the mountains glow with the pink reflection for which legend says they were named.

From the bridge to Zia Road, your turnaround point, the distance is exactly one mile. This is an open, expansive stretch, good for walking briskly and loosening up. Here, Santa Fe Trail goes straight south, undulating with the terrain. There are no specific landmarks, just panoramic scenery and a country feeling. Most of the homes along this part of Old Santa Fe Trail are set far back from the road and hidden in the pinons. When you reach Sun Mountain Road, exactly half a mile from the bridge, you'll be able to enjoy a sweeping view of plains, buttes and mesas to the Southwest. As you observe the skyline, one mountain stands out above all: Tetilla Peak. Its breast-like shape inspired its name. Tetilla Peak has long held importance in the religious life of Indians.

Look to the roadside as well—a microcosm at your feet. In summer, a plethora of wildflowers flourishes along this part of Old Santa Fe Trail. Year-round, you'll be brushed on both sides of the road by large, bushy growths of *chamisa*. This native plant characterizes the fields and roadsides of all northern New Mexico, and it changes with the seasons. In winter and fall, it is an ash gray, tannish hue; in early summer, more a dusty olive; and in early fall it is abloom with countless small golden flowers. Lovely to look at, but don't make the mistake of picking them. The smell of these blossoms is as foul as the color is sweet.

A word of caution: As there are no streetlights, this walk is riskier at dusk. The stretch along Santa Fe Trail from the bridge to Zia Road, while still in city limits, has such a country feeling that some motorists speed. Wear reflective strips or clothing, or a luminous vest if you plan to walk or run here in the evening. Be alert to the occasional madman behind the wheel. Most of the time, however, it is fairly peaceful.

Walk to Zia Road, which will intersect with Santa Fe Trail on your right, turn around and head back to St. John's College. The same view, as you walk south to north, will look amazingly different. From Zia Road to the bridge, as you'll recall, is exactly a mile. It is a mile well known to many runners, for it happens to be one of the flattest you can find in Santa Fe. Before a local race, you will see runners timing themselves along the Bridge-to-Zia mile.

For very early risers, this particular mile often affords a sunrise symphony of indescribable pinks, delicate golds and peaches, set against hues of gray and purple. For evening walkers, the sunset viewed from this mile reveals an explosion of gold, orange and blue, and finally a valley full of twinkling lights- the city lighting up for the evening hours.

After you've reached the bridge, follow Old Santa Fe Trail to the intersection with Camino del Monte Sol that curves off to the right. Take Camino del Monte Sol, pass Mount Carmel Road, then turn right up Camino de Cruz Blanca. Walk uphill to the driveway leading to St. John's College, which is clearly visible on your right. You'll be retracing your steps if you did not take the arroyo route option. You'll recognize the track and tennis courts on your right, and cross over the arroyo viaduct on the way back to the campus.

GUADALUPE STREET LOOP

The Guadalupe Street district, a remarkable pocket of Santa Fe, grew up in conjunction with the railroad activity of the late 1800s and early 1900s. For the past decade, this neighborhood has been enjoying a commercial renaissance, with former residences, warehouses and flophouses being turned into bookstores, clothing boutiques, galleries, fine craft shops, restaurants, as well as a delicatessen, gourmet shop, theatre, frame store, pottery studio, and so on. When I first moved to Santa Fe in the 1960s, Guadalupe Street and its environs appeared rundown and shabby. Today, because of renovation and a general sprucing up, the area appears most inviting. In addition to all the creative new enterprises, the area also contains the State Records Center and Archives, the historic Santuario de Guadalupe church and part of the "Chile Line" railroad route, as well as several interesting residences and other buildings, a few plaqued by the Historic Santa Fe Foundation.

The Guadalupe walk is comprised of a gentle, flat two-mile loop that takes you from the historic railroad center, through the Guadalupe neighborhood, over the Santa Fe River and northward as far as Rio Grande Avenue and St. Catherine's Indian School. If possible, try to take this jaunt on the third Thursday of the month. That's when the Pinckney Tully House on Grant Avenue is officially open to visitors. (Hours

The former "University of New Mexico," now an office complex.

are normally from 9 a.m. till 5 p.m., but it would be wise to check first with the Historic Santa Fe Foundation.) You might begin the day with a tour of the Santuario de Guadalupe, and after the walk plan to have lunch at one of Guadalupe neighborhood's several restaurants. Another possibility is to take a picnic lunch to enjoy at one of the DeVargas Park picnic tables.

Begin at the intersection of Guadalupe and Garfield streets, about a half-mile southwest of the Plaza. The sandy-colored, mission-style Atchison, Topeka and Santa Fe Railway depot is set back from Guadalupe Street, and the brick-faced former Denver and Rio Grande Western Railway station is right on Guadalupe Street, a few paces to the left of the Santa Fe depot. The D. & R.G.W. station has been converted into a restaurant. Warehouses in the area bear further witness to Guadalupe Street's connection with the railroads. There is ample parking near the various depots and warehouses.

Before embarking on your walk, take a moment to go into the Atchison, Topeka and Santa Fe depot. Used for regular passenger service on a spur from the main line at Lamy, New Mexioo, until 1928, the depot served weekly "tour specials" even after that. Loads of up to 200 passengers would come up on the spur to Santa Fe and then be driven about such highlights as San Miguel Church, the Plaza area museums, and the Laboratory of Anthropology. It has been decades, however, since the last passengers came up on this spur; today's twice-a-day incoming freight cars bring lumber, building materials, and beer for local distributors. Outgoing cargoes are likely to include scoria, or volcanic landscaping rock, which is quarried far out on Airport Road, and pumice to be used in the making of soap or toothpaste.

Before you leave the Railway Yards, take special note of the style not only of the Atchison, Topeka and Santa Fe depot, but of the homes and buildings on adjacent side streets. Their California Spanish mission style was used by the Atchison, Topeka and Santa Fe company throughout the Southwest. It is also a unifying characteristic throughout the Guadalupe Street area.

Directly across from the depots, on Guadalupe and facing Garfield Street, is another historic landmark. Now used for stores and offices, the tall (by Santa Fe standards) cocoa-hued building with a tin roof was an early "University of New Mexico." The history of what turned out to be an ambitious but only mildly successful venture is one of the more fascinating aspects of the Guadalupe area.

After the end of the Civil War, church-related educational activity in New Mexico accelerated. The

47

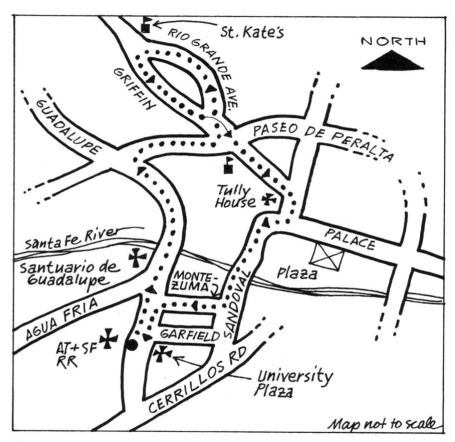

St. Kate's

RIO GRANDE AVE.

GRIFFIN

GUADALUPE

NORTH

PASEO DE PERALTA

Tully House

santa Fe River

Santuario de Guadalupe

PALACE

Plaza

MONTE-ZUMA

SANDOVAL

AGUA FRIA

AT+SF RR

GARFIELD

University Plaza

CERRILLOS RD

Map not to scale

founding of "The University of New Mexico at Santa Fe" was the work of an energetic Congregationalist, Rev. Horatio O. Ladd. In 1880, The New West Education Commission sent Reverend Ladd to be the director of a certain Santa Fe Academy. Ladd, who brought his wife and son with him, found Santa Fe extremely grubby and unpleasant. He referred to it as a "rough, western mining region" and complained that because of the darkness of Santa Fe's long, low adobes, he was unable to find the town's traders or lawyers after nightfall.

Ladd did not get along with local school officials, so by 1881 he had founded his own school, the so-called "University New Mexico." Its declared purpose was to provide a Protestant Christian education to this benighted area, and to aid the Territory's moral development. Money was a constant problem for the fledgling school, and Ladd held the first classes in his home. There were 67 students and three departments (primary, intermediate, and academic). Tuition was $3 a month.

Enrollment had picked up by 1882, so Reverend Ladd optimistically started work on a building for his learning institution. Finally completed in 1887, Whitin Hall (at the corner of Guadalupe and Garfield) was a three-story, red brick building with classrooms and a 25-student dormitory. The name "Whitin" was chosen because of a $13,500 memorial gift given by the family of John C. Whitin in Massachusetts. In the meantime, Reverend Ladd had begun an Indian school department and founded The Ramona School. In order to finance this addition to his educational complex, he solicited funds from sources as diverse as a church in Toledo, Ohio, to President Cleveland. In 1885, when The Ramona School opened, there were 33 boys and 11 girls, all Pueblo Indians. After the opening of St. Catherine's Industrial School for Indians in 1887, all Pueblo students began attending that institution, and The Ramona School took only girls from the Apache reservations.

Apparently Ladd wearied of the struggle, for in 1887 he handed over the schools to another Congregational minister, a Reverend Hood. By 1888, the New West Education Commission had taken control of the struggling "University," and by 1893 it had become Santa Fe High School. In the 1920s, the building became The Franciscan Hotel, and it later served as St. Mary's Convent and then eventually the Garfield Apartments, a notorious flophouse in the 1960s. The renovation and conversion to University Plaza took place in 1978.

Now head north on Guadalupe Street. Just beyond the railroad area you will pass the State Records Center and Archives building, enhanced on its east side by a vividly painted multi-cultural mural. After getting a good view from afar, cross the street for a more detailed study. This extraordinary creation was donated in 1980 by artists Rosemary Stearns, Gilberto Guzman, David Bradley, Frederico Vigil, and Zara Kriegstein. The artists and the topics of the mural are tri-cultural, representing Native Americans, Hispanics and Anglos.

Remember, this is a short walk, so you can feel free to linger. The mural is intended to show New Mexico's development through several stages. On the far left, you'll note medicine men, a bull, and a depiction of the coming of the railroad. The center shows New Mexico's first settlers, the corn goddess holding a test tube and a microscope, and a mysterious face looking in both directions; the left half of the face is female, the right, male. At the bottom of the center section is a New Mexico fiesta scene. The far right of the mural, dramatizing the conflict between science and ecology, portrays the possible future: It shows a deeply eroded gorge cut through the countryside. Whatever you think of the quality of this work, it is uniquely New Mexican.

Want to browse through the State Archives? You can. Most of the resources there are available to the public. You'll find records, maps, photographs, and books concerning topics from land grants to geneaology. Archive hours (at this writing) are from 8 a.m. till 5 p.m., Monday through Friday. You must sign in and out when visiting.

There is good sidewalk along both sides of Guadalupe. Continue north on either the left or the right. You will shortly pass by another example of Spanish Mission architecture: the former D. I. Miller and Co. Cracker Factory, most recently a car body shop. Within the same block is an old stone warehouse, now a shop for cooking equipment. Built in the 1880s, the warehouse is the oldest stone structure used for business purposes in the city. It belonged to various Spanish and Anglo families, and has also served as a Coca-Cola bottling plant and an art gallery.

Keep in mind that you're now retracing the route of the Denver and Rio Grande Western Railway, as it wended its way through Santa Fe. It travelled directly down the middle of street. Old photographs show the Denver and Rio Grande line passing in front of the Santuario de Guadalupe church.

The first railroad line, the A.T.&S.F. spur, came to Santa Fe in 1880. In 1886, the Denver and Rio Grande met the Santa Fe at the Railroad Yards on Guadalupe Street. The D.&R.G.W. route from Santa Fe up the Rio Grande to Colorado was called the "Chile Line", because it served New Mexico's agricultural heartland. The narrow gauge line was abandoned and the rails torn up shortly before World War II.

Continue north up Guadalupe, and you will soon reach the Santuario de Guadalupe on your left. At this prominent location on the south bank of the Santa Fe River are actually two churches nested together. In the foreground is the ancient, restored adobe shrine to Our Lady of Guadalupe; behind it the modern Guadalupe Church, built in 1961. The historic church, which dates from about 1777, is regarded as the oldest extant building created to honor Our Lady of Guadalupe, who is the patron saint of Mexico and much of Latin America. The edifice was altered many times throughout its history, and its present form is the result of a mid-1970s restoration. Because of the Guadalupe Historic Foundation's efforts and many private and public grants, the shrine was brought back to the form and character it possessed in the eighteenth century.

Today the Santuario is used for dramatic, musical and artistic presentations appropriate to Hispanic culture and the nature of the church itself. Chamber music performances are frequently scheduled here. The acoustics are exceptional. Take time to go inside and wander through the standing exhibit which explains the church's history and restoration, and absorb the tranquil effects of soft lighting and thick adobe walls. Dwell a bit upon the Santuario's past, its importance as parish church for surrounding families, and its place near the end of the *Camino Real*, the ancient road connecting Santa Fe with Chihuahua, Mexico. The carved vigas, hardwood floors, eighteenth-century oil paintings and the sanctuary's Mexican altarpiece of the Blessed Virgin all lead to a lovely impression of warmth and serenity.

A special guided tour of the Santuario may be arranged by calling ahead to the Guadalupe Historic Foundation. You'll get a deeper understanding of the church's background, including the features of the Bishop Lamy room. The Santuario is open 9:00 a.m. to 4:00 p.m. Monday through Saturday and noon through 4:00 p.m. on Sunday, except in winter, when it is closed on weekends. Admission is free.

After your visit to the Santuario de Guadalupe, cross the bridge over the Santa Fe River. To your right, across the street from the Santuario, is DeVargas Park. This park has become the scene for such typical Santa Fe community events as the 1982 "Nobody for President" rally, as well as rock concerts and serious political campaigning. You may wish to come back here for a picnic lunch.

After you cross the bridge, cross Alameda Street and continue north up Guadalupe for several blocks until you come to Paseo de Peralta. At this point, you will have covered a mile.

Even though you may get into some heavy traffic

along this stretch of Guadalupe, there are sidewalks which make walking very convenient. Pass by the back of the low Hilton Hotel and a mix of Santa Fe businesses. Your will come to Paseo de Peralta and a broad intersection with lights. To the north across the four-lane Paseo you'll see DeVargas Shopping Center and fascinating old Rosario Chapel and cemetery. Turn right and walk east (toward the Sangre de Cristo mountains) along Paseo de Peralta. At Griffin Street, take a left across Paseo de Peralta. Across Peralta and a small arroyo, Griffin will soon fork. Keep to the right, Rio Grande Avenue, and proceed to the entrance of St. Catherine's Indian School. (For more about the school, see the **St. Catherine's Run** chapter.)

As you approach "St. Kate's", as it's usually called, you'll enjoy a good view of the main red-roofed classroom building, the oldest edifice on campus. Instead of entering the school grounds, take a hairpin turn left back on to Griffin and walk back on the dirt road to Paseo de Peralta. Cross Peralta and continue south on Griffin Street.

The other side of Griffin is but a short twig, and it soon shortly feeds into Grant Avenue and a block which includes the Pinckney Tully House and the A.M. Bergere House, both of which have been plaqued by the Historic Santa Fe Foundation. Before you reach the juncture of Griffin and Grant, you'll pass by the Santa Fe Judicial Complex, one of many examples of downtown urban renewal. This building used to be Leah Harvey Junior High School (where I taught eighth grade reading in one of the ground floor classrooms). In the 1970s, it was abandoned as a school, gutted out and rebuilt, and converted to its present use as a modern court house complex.

On the "Y" of the Griffin-Grant Street juncture is a large, attractive Pueblo style Presbyterian church. This is the oldest Protestant church in New Mexico. On your right, as Griffin melds into Grant, is the Pinckney R. Tully House, built in 1851 and restored in 1974 by the Historic Santa Fe Foundation. Its bright red simulated (painting) brick exterior represents a style that enjoyed great popularity during the 1890s. It was an effort to make Santa Fe adobes look more "American". The long, low former home contains ten rooms. It was built by Pinckney Tully, son of a French-Canadian trader. When Tully and his family moved to the Mesilla Valley, the house was passed on to other traders. It has served as the home of several prominent Santa Feans and for a time in the twentieth century, was used for apartments. Today the Tully House is the office of a law firm, reflecting the "gentrifica--tion" of downtown Santa Fe in recent years.

Cross Grant Avenue to the former home of Alfred Maurice Bergere. It's a stately two-story, balconied edifice set back amidst large trees and a lush lawn. Built in the 1870s for officers quarters, the Bergere House came to be as part of the Fort Marcy military reservation. Of six houses built in this neighborhood for such purposes, it is one of two still extant. (The other is the Hewett House, behind the Fine Arts Museum.) Bergere, an Englishman of Italian ancestry, occupied the house after the U.S. Army abandoned Fort Marcy. The house has been altered considerably. The original cross-gabled roof of the main section was removed in 1926 and replaced with a squared Spanish-Pueblo style top level. The Bergere House is also now used as an office building.

Continue walking south on Grant Avenue, noting the striking building beyond Tully House, at the corner of Johnson and Grant. Now a bed and breakfast inn, this stately brick home first belonged to a ranching family, the Windsors. It was constructed around 1903. In 1912, it was purchased by Judge Robinson, who lived there with his family for over 20 years.

The next block along Grant is filled by the Pueblo-style Santa Fe County Courthouse. Grant ends at a main thoroughfare, where Palace Avenue becomes Sandoval Street. Turn right here. There is an ample sidewalk around the heavily trafficked left-hand curve which will take you back to another river crossing. A block before the river, at the southwest corner of Sandoval and West San Francisco, you'll pass a Territorial-style commercial building, dating from the 1700s, which used to be the Ortiz family estate. It's now part of the Hilton Hotel complex. Continuing south, you'll pass once more through DeVargas Park. Continue on Sandoval to Montezuma Street. Turn right on Montezuma and take it one block back to Guadalupe Street. Take a left on Guadalupe, cross the street, and you will be once more back at the Railroad Yards.

Alto Street Neighborhood

ALTO / ALAMEDA / AGUA FRIA LOOP

This walk gives one a cross section of residential areas of Santa Fe that developed later than the Plaza area—and that are still growing. It's as flat a walk as you'll find in the city. It's paved too, making this a relatively smooth and easy trek. Depending on "extras" (such as the stroll around Bicentennial Park), it will be about 4½ miles. If you're in the mood for a longer walk, you can go farther into the country on West Alameda or do a more thorough exploration of the river bed bordering the south side of Santa Fe River Road.

This is a nice walk if you're ready for a refreshing contrast from the downtown area. Instead of trendy boutiques and new galleries, you'll encounter a community garden, a tortilla factory, some middle income housing, a feed store, and a small neighborhood shopping center. You'll find a generally harmonious blend of homes and shops, but the dominant feeling of the walk is "residential." The Rio Vista subdivision, out on West Alameda, used to be considered quite in the country. Now it is rapidly filling in with small, often attractive houses. Growth in this area, while steady and rapid, does not seem to be either as contrived or as frantic as it is elsewhere. And most of the growth is sheerly residential.

You'll begin and end in Bicentennial Park on Alto

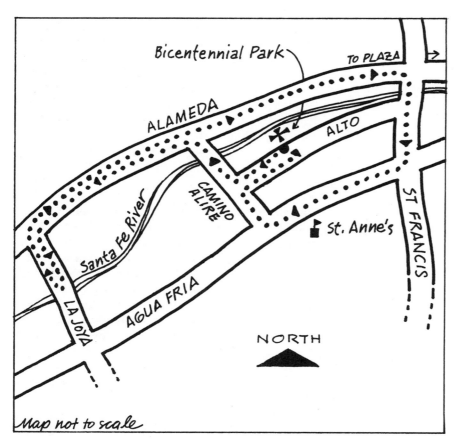

Bicentennial Park

TO PLAZA

ALAMEDA

ALTO

CAMINO ALIRE

Santa Fe River

St. Anne's

ST FRANCIS

LA JOYA

AGUA FRIA

NORTH

Map not to scale

Street. It's on the part of Alto west of St. Francis Drive. Dedicated in 1975, the 22-acre plot includes picnic tables, baseball and football fields, and tennis courts, as well as the city's only outdoor public swimming pool. Before it became a park, the land was used for a few homes and a large lumber yard.

Before you begin your walk, here's a bit of history about the *Barrio de Guadalupe*. The area which includes today's walk was one of Santa Fe's Spanish Colonial neighborhoods. Its name comes from the Guadalupe Church, licensed in 1795 by the Bishop of Durango. According to the *Santa Fe Historic Neighborhood Study,* published by the city in 1988, "The 1823 census and tax returns listed 57 families in the Barrio de Guadalupe; the most common occupations were farmer and laborer, with a scattering of masons, cobblers, tailors, shepherds, and silversmiths. The 1841 Mexican census show a substantial gain in population for the neighborhood."

During the 1880s, the Barrio was greatly affected by the arrival of the railroad, and by 1912 Santa Fe city planners announced that the area should become a factory region. But warehouses and small, modest homes increasingly filled the narrow streets.

Here also is the Alto Street Center, former scene of the summer and fall Farmer's Market that now takes place in the Sanbusco Center on Montezuma Street. The Alto Center, which flanks Bicentennial Park's fields, consists of three light gray cement block structures. The building to the far left (as you face the complex) houses a family medical and dental center. The middle structure is the walled-in outdoor swimming pool. During the summer, the pool is open to the public for a nominal daily or monthly fee. The building to the right of the pool is the Mary Esther Gonzales Senior Citizens Center.

Tarry a bit longer in the park to stroll about in the long, wide strip of grassy field that begins behind the Alto Center. Bordered by the Santa Fe River bed and Alto Street, it offers a refreshing strip of green space within the closed-in and fast-growing city all around. One of the loveliest features of Bicentennial Park is the view to the east of the Sangre de Cristos. What's more, this peaceful park is seldom crowded.

Leaving the grassy fields of the park, return to Alto Street and go southwest away from the Center. This part of Alto is relatively new, having been developed and re-aligned in the seventies to provide access to the park. When you reach Camino Alire, turn right. There's an interesting contrast between the two housing developments on either side of the street: To your left is a cluster of Santa Fe style townhouses, to the right a series of large, blockish apartments which make up a government rent supplement project. There is a sidewalk along this section, which takes you across the river bed to West Alameda.

Turn left on Alameda, a broad street that runs through the city along the north side of the river. Although there is usually running water at the River Park downtown, the Santa Fe River here is generally a dry bed. Later on, you'll have access to the river bed, a great place for studying land formation and natural and human ecology. Head west, passing on your right such streets as Sam, Moore, Ephriam and San Salvador in the rather humble residential Torreon Addition. Take care to keep within the boundaries of the narrow, sandy shoulder. The traffic here is fairly heavy and there's no sidewalk.

Shortly, a large sign on your left announces Rio Vista, the new subdivision. Turn left on La Joya and walk gradually downhill exactly 1/10 mile to Santa Fe River Road. At this point, including your stroll through the park, you'll have covered about a mile. In the broad, normally dry river bed which borders Santa Fe River Road, you may be tempted to add as much as a half mile more.

Climb down the banks and walk up or down the arroyo as far as time and inclination allow. The sandy floor is soft and cushiony, and the terrain is marked with interesting rocks, occasional rusted pieces of autos and other discarded remnants of modern life. Along the river bed you will see primitive roads which climb either side. (Obviously, the people who live along the ridges became impatient with having to drive all the way to a bridge to cross to the other side.) Though car traffic is infrequent, a truck occasionally lumbers across the dry bed, down and then up the makeshift crossing. This area is, in fact, an odd but typically New Mexican combination of road, footpath and dumping ground.

When you've had enough of the river bed, wend your way back to civilization. Now head back the opposite direction on Alameda, east toward town and facing the Sangre de Cristos. Stay on West Alameda past the Camino Alire intersection. There are many lovely trees along this stretch—weeping willows, towering poplars—as well as an interesting hodgepodge of homes. Some are old and established, with tended, grassy front lawns and an occasional birdbath or religious statue for adornment. Mixed in are some mobile homes, with perhaps a few dilapidated cars and trucks in the dusty yard. No specific style predominates, and yet the overall effect is very Santa Fean.

There is a small stuccoed building on the corner of Alameda and Alire that has served as a neighborhood grocery, then as a religious meeting place. Most recently, it's become a glass and mirror company.

Many of the winding streets on your left, north off Alameda, are named after the trees which line them. This is the gracious Casa Solana subdivision, one of the earliest planned neighborhoods in the city. You'll pass a feed store on the right, and shortly after that Casa Solana Shopping Center, a gas station and elementary school on your left. Soon West Alameda intersects with busy, four-lane St. Francis Drive. Turn right (south) here.

Use the sidewalk along St. Francis as traffic can be heavy and fast here. With so many quiet areas in Santa Fe, I am reluctant to advise walking along a busy thoroughfare such as St. Francis, but for today's course it's necessary. After just a mile, take another right at Agua Fria Street.

On Agua Fria you'll find yourself able to proceed in more leisurely fashion. Unlike the walled-in sections of Santa Fe, many yards in this area are open. There is definitely a neighborhood feeling here. On the right, you'll pass a community garden plot, densely and productively planted during the growing season by people who live and work in this neighborhood. Further up the street, on your left, you'll pass by a tortilla factory and then St. Anne's School. Look closely and you may see the pitched roof of St. Anne Parish church just to the south. Consider detouring on Alicia Street to stroll around this very different piece of Santa Fe architecture. Return to Agua Fria and continue west one more block to Camino Alire.

Turn right on Camino Alire, and after a short downhill stroll, take another right on Alto Street, whereupon you'll soon be back at the Alto Street Center. Depending on how much you have wandered in the park and in the Santa Fe River bed, you'll have covered between 4½ and 5 miles. If it is summer and the Farmer's Market is still in progress, you'll no doubt be tempted to buy some fruits and vegetables to take home with you.

Eli Levin 82

NORTHWEST QUADRANT COUNTRY WALK

Characterized by pinon and juniper covered hills, peaceful trails and roads, and a pristine sense of natural expanse, the Northwest Quadrant of Santa Fe is one of the city's loveliest stretches in which to take a scenic walk. Today's outing, a four-mile 'V", consists of one mile out and back along a high ridge overlooking the city and another leg, about the same length, on an undulating county road that runs due north.

Though future developments will be changing this section of Santa Fe, it is now empty and serene. Here, one feels "in the country", away from the hubbub of downtown or the strip development of the city's southwest. The only sounds you're likely to hear are the wind rustling the pinons and junipers, the brushing of your own stride against the chamisa, or the flutter of a jay or grackle. Your only company may be an occasional darting lizard.

Between the two roads I direct you to take (the path above the park and County Road 85) runs Buckman Road, named for an old community, once used as a movie set, out near the Rio Grande. The town of Buckman lived and died some twenty miles northwest of Santa Fe. Also located in this territory were the original road to Taos and the tracks of the "Chile Line". If you wander far enough beyond the city you'll see some pilings of the old railroad. And as in other parts of the city, there has been archeological activity

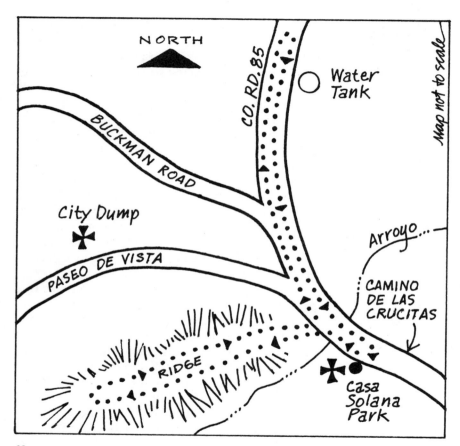

NORTH

CO. RD. 85

Water Tank

Map not to scale

BUCKMAN ROAD

City Dump

PASEO DE VISTA

Arroyo...

CAMINO DE LAS CRUCITAS

RIDGE

Casa Solana Park

in this area over the years.

Casa Solana Park, complete with tennis courts, baseball field and some of the city's more imaginative playground equipment (a wooden bridge on stilts, drainage pipe forts, a climber made of inner tubes) is your point of origin for today's walking. It's on Camino de las Crucitas, which takes off from North St. Francis Drive. There is a small lot where you can leave your car. Perched on a knoll above the park is a cement table with benches where you might enjoy a picnic lunch after walking. There's also a water pump by a nearby cottonwood tree.

Face the playground area of the park and clamber up the dirt embankment behind it, keeping to the left. You'll find yourself on a narrow, one-lane dirt road. This will be the main thread of your hike out a ridge overlooking the city. There are trails next to and interwoven with the road, and it doesn't really matter which one you take. Just be sure to stay at the top of the ridge.

Hike out for 15 or 20 minutes along this "shelf" overlooking downtown Santa Fe. Be sure to look backwards before you begin for a splendid prospect of the Sangre de Cristos. As you walk along the ridge, you'll enjoy a panorama of mountains all around, and the rooftops and city landmarks of Santa Fe below. It's a good place for binoculars.

When you've walked about one-third of a mile out, you'll have a good view of part of the Northwest Quadrant area, some of it now flattened and cleared for development. Remember to stay on the highest point of the ridge. Stay in the "center" as much as possible: wandering off to the left will bring you too much downhill.

Amble on until you come to a point where there is a definite downhill. If you went any further, you'd end up on the asphalt streets below. Here is where you turn around and head back the opposite direction. Now you'll be treated to a magnificent, unobstructed view of the Sangre de Cristo mountains ahead and to your right. At the far end and peeking over closer peaks is Santa Fe Baldy. In the center of this mountain cluster is the Santa Fe Ski Basin. To the far right are Picacho and Atalaya Peaks, then the lower Sun and Moon mountains.

The uppermost reaches of this range are snow-covered for at least half the year. In good seasons, the ski area you see has excellent powder snow from November through April. Ski conditions often remain good well into May or even June, but downhill skiing stops toward the end of April due to a time-limiting agreement between the ski resort and the National Forest Service. Cross-country skiing can go on for a few weeks longer.

Continue returning along your ridgetop route back to Solana Park. By now you'll have walked two miles and may be ready for a short stop before taking the second prong of this two-part outing. If you've started in late morning, it may be time for a bite here before you start out again.

After your rest or repast, walk to the parking lot and take a lefthand turn. Soon the asphalt will end and you'll find yourself on a dirt road. Several non-named paths and roads will veer off to the left. Keep to the right to avoid being sidetracked. After about one tenth of a mile, you'll see Paseo de Vista on your left, announced by a sign that points toward the city landfill (the street's name is not on the sign). Shortly after this road, the beginning of Buckman Road forks off on the left, and then finally you'll come to County Road 85.

Here is the real beginning of the second out-and-back part of your walk. While the first leg of today's journey was wide open, this road is closed in on both sides by thick growths of pinon and juniper. There are several arroyos, as well as splendid mountain vistas.

Three large arroyos will intersect your path. The first comes about half a mile after you've left Solana Park. Like many arroyos around the outskirts of town, it contains old cars, stray mattress springs, and sun-dry broken and discarded objects. But in addition to debris, you'll see all kinds of interesting quartz formations and fragments. During warm months, the arroyos are lined with a variety of wildflowers. You're likely to see an occasional lizard, beetle, and other harmless critters. If you're not in a hurry, take a few side-trips into the arroyos. The peace of these places and the simple pleasure of walking on sand make arroyo digressions worthwhile.

After the first arroyo, you'll hike uphill about a tenth of a mile before encountering the next dip. Here, at approximately one mile from Solana Park, you'll encounter a second arroyo. To your right will be a particularly lovely view of the Sangre de Cristos. During the winter months, when snow blankets the high mountain peaks, the contrast between dark green pinons in the foreground and the white peaks in the background is breathtaking. After enjoying the view from this arroyo vantage point, ascend once more on the next gentle rise.

This is a relatively "uneventful" walk, and allows one plenty of time and energy for reflection. Perhaps because Santa Fe is arid, I sometimes find myself thinking of bodies of water when I walk in this countryside. I always draw a mental analogy between the distant mesas and plains and the ocean. A number of artists have depicted such an imaginary phenomenon in their paintings. To carry the water daydreams still further, envision this main road as a river passageway, with the arroyos its tributaries cutting off to either side.

After the rise, you'll find that the road is narrower than before, and deeper cut. Look to the left for a view of the Jemez mountains. Local gardeners say that when the snow has disappeared from its peaks, it is time to plant vegetables. Ahead to your right is a water storage tank. In another half mile, you will reach the third arroyo, the deepest and most dramatic so far.

After you've been on County Road 85 for just about a mile you'll see a Pueblo Service Company high-tension tower. It is set back from the road and on the right. This is a convenient turnaround point, although you may wish to wander on quite a bit further. If you're adventuresome, you'll be tempted to follow the road over the next rise, and the next—but be aware of the time you've allowed yourself and your own walking comfort.

As you head back toward the park, you'll be treated again to now familiar and yet always exhilirating mountain panoramas. Although there is little vehicular traffic here, and this is generally a peaceful and safe excursion, I shouldn't omit mentioning the dog problem. Santa Fe has quite a few strays running in packs, and although efforts to control these animals have reportedly intensified, they still pose a menace. I have talked with walkers on this route who have been occasionally bothered. If you see or hear dogs, it would be a good idea to arm yourself with a stick or a big rock or two. Usually, just the show of a stick or rock is sufficient to keep dogs at a safe distance. They've learned from experience what "weapons" are for.

Beyond the public utilities area, you will find more tempting arroyos. Explore if you wish, but remember to return the way you came. The repetitive features in this landscape could get you temporarily lost. When it's finally time to turn back, just retrace your steps back on County Road 85, then down on Camino de las Crucitas until you are once again at Solana Park.

E.G. Serm 1982

The Belloli House

ALAMEDA /
UPPER CANYON /
CERRO GORDO
WALK

The loop formed by today's walk—Alameda Street, Upper Canyon Road, and Cerro Gordo Road—is equally well-suited to walking and running and includes a lovely variety of terrain. This 3½-mile route ranges from broad, paved, tree-lined Alameda to narrow, picturesque Canyon, to the rural, hilly dirt Cerro Gordo stretch. There are two parks, but neither drinking water nor public restrooms along the way. Since the Cerro Gordo stretch is unpaved, you'd be better off doing this one when there is no chance of mud or snow conditions. Few things make walking more unpleasant than clumping along with a pound of mud clinging to the cleats of your hiking boots or soles of your canvas walkers. Because of the many tall shade trees along Alameda and Canyon, this route makes an excellent summertime excursion.

It is a relatively short walk, although one with fascinating visual interest. There are pauses planned at Cristo Rey Church and Cerro Gordo Park. Because it's not long, I suggest you start out in mid-morning. That way you'll arrive at Cerro Gordo Park about the right time for a picnic lunch. More about this natural, high desert park later...

Begin today's hike at Patrick Smith Park on East Alameda, a few blocks east of the intersection of Alameda and Palace Avenue. Better known as "Canyon Road Park", it is a large, grassy strip that lies be-

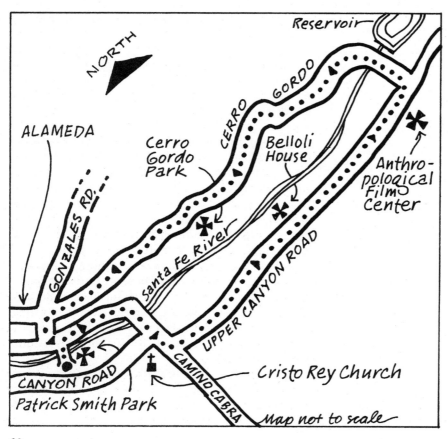

NORTH

Reservoir

CERRO GORDO

ALAMEDA

Cerro Gordo Park

Belloli House

Anthropological Film Center

GONZALES RD.

Santa Fe River

UPPER CANYON ROAD

CAMINO CABRA

CANYON ROAD

Patrick Smith Park

Cristo Rey Church

Map not to scale

tween East Alameda and Canyon Road, and is used for baseball and soccer practice. It is also a favored gathering spot for teenagers in their low-riders. There are climbers, swings and a basketball court, all of which makes it one of the city's more populated parks. As you will discover, the other park on today's route offers a remarkable contrast with its quietude and air of isolation.

If you have driven up to Patrick Smith Park, you'll leave your car in the paved lot. Lock up your car securely and then backtrack on foot, recrossing the concrete bridge over the Santa Fe River to East Alameda. Take a right. East Alameda is graced with some of the city's tallest and oldest cottonwoods. Opposite the park are several large estates; the homes are set back from the street and surrounded by exceptionally lush lawns and shrubbery. Because of high water rates and the relative scarcity of water, large grass lawns in Santa Fe are somewhat of an anomaly.

As you walk the tenth of a mile to the end of Alameda, you have no sidewalk but there is plenty of room, nonetheless, for both cars and pedestrians. At the end of Alameda, several roads—Camino Pequeno, Canyon, and Camino Cabra—all gather. Take a right once more, walking uphill on Cabra and across the river again until you come to Cristo Rey Church. Planned by master architect John Gaw Meem and associate Hugo Zehner, and built in 1939-40, Cristo Rey is reputedly the largest adobe structure in the United States. Its conception arose from the need for a more conveniently located neighborhood church. Parishioners who lived on Canyon Road and Cerro Gordo used to have to trudge into town to St. Francis Cathedral to attend masses and other parish functions. Cristo Rey was also built as a part of memorial to the Coronado Cuarto Centennial, commemorating the 400th anniversary of Coronado's trek through the Southwest in 1539. Find an unlocked door (usually one under the portal along the south side) and walk inside.

His Excellency, Reverend R. A. Gerken, then the Archbishop of Santa Fe, was responsible for inclusion of the striking *reredos* in Cristo Rey's nave. The stone altarpiece is massive: over 30 feet tall and 18 feet wide. It's considered one of the more remarkable pieces of ecclestical art in the area. It depicts saints revered for centuries as well as those newly canonized. Details are both Mexican and Indian. Evidence of New World origins may be found in the feather headdresses worn by cherubs and kneeling figures. Fashioned from white rock found in Jacona, New Mexico, the altarpiece was made in Santa Fe by Mexican workmen.

Our Lady of Light is portrayed at the center of the *reredos*, which calls to mind its "known" history. Built during the 1700's, the *reredos* was a central decoration in the military chapel (the Church of Our Lady of Light) which stood on the Plaza's south side from 1750 till 1859. Apparently, Francisco Antonio Marin del Valle, governor and capitan-general from 1754-1760, donated the piece to the little military chapel.

In 1869, after *La Castrense,* Santa Fe's main adobe church, had been torn down to make way for St. Francis Cathedral, Archbishop Lamy removed the *reredos* to the latter. It remained undisplayed, stored behind the main altar of St. Francis Cathedral, until Archbishop Gerken selected it to grace the new Cristo Rey Church. Now, it is not only seen, it is the celebrated centerpiece of the church. The high windows facing Cristo Rey's east side flood the *reredos* with light, where it provides a dramatic backdrop for masses held there. Because of its soft lighting, openness and simplicity, the massive interior of the church engenders a feeling of peace and solace.

Cristo Rey is a masterpiece of native materials. The adobe bricks are of mud mixed at the site; the interior ceiling of split cedars is from the area; and the wooden corbels are handcarved by local woodworkers. The doors, pews, confessionals and vestment cases were crafted in Santa Fe, specifically for this church. Cristo Rey's wrought iron fixtures were all made by boys at Lourdes Trade School in Albuquerque.

From the outside, Cristo Rey seems at times almost like an earthen sculpture. Its towers look toward the Sangre de Cristos, reaching and aspiring. Yet the adobe mass and generally long, low lines make it appear to be clinging to the earth.

Next door to Cristo Rey is the old Manderfield School, now headquarters for Operation Head Start and the neighborhood polling place.

Directly across from Cristo Rey is the continuation of your walk: upper Canyon Road, inviting you upward towards the foothills of the Sangre de Cristos. Note the road-sign at this juncture. You must make a sharp left. Upper Canyon is narrow and tree-lined, hence visibility for oncoming traffic is minimal. Keep your eyes and ears open. It is pleasantly paved and curbless, permitting you to step easily out of the way of occasional traffic. Upper Canyon starts out with an uphill jaunt, notched with small side roads cutting off to the right. Like the lower Canyon Road, it has been home for citizens of Santa Fe's art community. Some of the studio homes along here are reminiscent of Santa Fe in earlier days, when artists resided and sold work in one place. Now many of these places are the homes of socialites.

After you've been walking for about a mile, you will see a rambling pink house on the left side of the road, a favorite subject of many a local artist. This is the Georgio Belloli house, built by the artist/sculptor/builder of the same name. Belloli made a hobby of renovating old houses long before it became fashionable. At one time he went to Mexico and restored an entire village. His Santa Fe residence, full of lavish wood carving inside, includes a patio complete with sculptures and a fountain, where Belloli was said to bathe both summer and winter. Belloli and his wife were pictured, in a 1948 *Saturday Evening Post* article about Santa Fe, dining on their patio.

Neighbors recall Georgio Belloli as a large, strong and well-built man who was frequently seen driving his one-horse shay to town before the sun hit the road. He was known for having "a great flair" and a lot of "style."

Let your eyes course over the beautifully tile fluted roof and the picturesque, almost gothic state of disrepair. It's easy to see why artists and photographers are drawn to capture the Belloli house. Yet it is just one of several styles of architecture you'll see on this walk.

As you traverse Santa Fe by foot you'll discover on closer observation that its homes are not all uniformly Pueblo adobe style, or a monotonous mix of the Pueblo and Territorial styles. True, those are the dominant architectural styles. But you will find also Victorian remnants, brick houses from the early 1900s, "ranch" styles, eclectic solar forms, and even delightful anomalies such as the aforementioned Italianate Belloli House.

On either side of the road you'll see an interesting assortment of beautiful old adobes, modern solar homes, coyote fences, adobe walls, curious variations on Southwestern themes, and a cross-river view to the next leg of your walk, the Cerro Gordo Road neighborhood.

Right before the end of the paved part of Upper Canyon, you'll reach the Anthropology Film Center on your right, a unique school for the study of visual anthropology.

Run by Carroll Williams and his wife Joan, the center was founded in 1965 and operates in conjunction with Temple University. The school is small and deliberately shuns publicity. It is limited to about 25 students a year. According to Williams, the kind of learning students do at the center enables them to record and spread the living anthropological record through media like public television and documentary motion pictures. The first semester teaches technology; the second is involved with independent projects. Its work serves the academic community all over the world.

By the end of the pavement on Upper Canyon Road, you will have walked about 1½ miles. A cluster of mailboxes on the left marks the point at which Cerro Gordo takes off from Canyon. Begin the next leg of your journey by making the left turn (north) here.

Upper Canyon Road does continue as a dirt lane a little further into the foothills, and you may be tempted to follow it. A sign or two discourages traffic here, but these are intended to keep this lovely area free of congestion. If you detour up this way, you'll be treated to to a prospect of Nichols Reservoir, the largest body of water anywhere near the city. Here's all the water that would naturally be flowing down the Santa Fe River. On your right you'll encounter the beautiful, rambling Randall Davey estate, former home of a celebrated painter, and now a facility of the Audubon Society. The road ends at a locked gate with foreboding signs—heed them and do not trespass into the fenced off area. The water company and the National Forest Service are stern about keeping people out of the upper Santa Fe River area. Backtrack down to the intersection with Cerro Gordo.

Cross over the small bridge just past the mailboxes and begin a dirt road adventure which includes dips, curves, flat stretches and wonderful views into the small valley that holds Santa Fe River. After a brief up and down, the road flattens out into a stretch of relatively level walking, until it begins downhill turns towards town. The walk is fairly easy all the way. Although there are occasional dogs and cars, Cerro Gordo is generally safe, peaceful, and almost rural in character.

Along this route, you'll be treated to Santa Fe's widest variety of architectural samples: crumbling old adobes, pink stuocoed frame homes, rambling communal dwellings, modern solar homes, and plenty of examples of owner-built inspirations. In true Santa Fe style, there are virtual palaces juxtaposed with very humble dwellings. Cerro Gordo is also a road of coyote and barbed wire fences, and walls made of wood, adobe and even fine stone work.

After you've walked 2½ miles on today's route, you'll come upon Cerro Gordo Park, a quiet spot that's perfect for enjoying a picnic lunch. The park is off the main road, down a steep drive that hooks back to the left. The park is fairly easy to miss. There's little to distinguish it from the open fields that border this side of the river. Perhaps because of this, at any given time you're likely to find that you're the only person there.

The solitude is glorious, however. It seems to invite one to explore this lovely, isolated stretch of public land. Watching over the park is a rustic wooden Saint Francis carved by Ben Ortega, a famous New Mexican *santero* (saint-maker). The good saint is gracefully weathering, and his hands have been missing for a couple of years. The surrounding land and vegetation are rugged and completely natural. A path leads to an open air pavilion and to the edge of the sudden dropoff down to the river plain. A view from this point is a must. Craggy boulders and *cholla* cacti cling to the top of the ledges. The rocks glisten with mica. Further down the ravine runs the Santa Fe River, almost completely obscured by abundant undergrowth. The flora of the river plain makes a striking contrast to the desert chamisa, juniper and range grasses of the park itself.

A 1909 issue of *The New Mexican* contains an account of the local school superintendent and his wife fishing in the Santa Fe River. It's hard to picture such an outing taking place today. True, during the spring runoff and summer thunderstorms the river flows deeper than its usual trickle. For the most part, however, the Santa Fe River is a mere spectre of its former self. The waters are held back upriver by Nichols and McClure Reservoirs, and are now the source of much of the city's water supply.

You will see several wrought-iron benches placed around the park. Pick one as a resting spot and break out your picnic. If you're inclined toward sketching or snoozing, this is an ideal setting. It's also a fine place to do a little reading if you've tucked a paperback novel in your pack. What I find most enjoyable in this setting is just meditating.

Along the east end of the park is the home of some other people who appreciate the meditative atmosphere of the area. The long, low building is occupied by a small band of Zen Buddhists. Within its walls stands a Tibetan Buddhist shrine, the first of its kind in the Western Hemisphere.

After your interlude of rest, climb the hill back up toward Cerro Gordo Road and continue onward. The looming hill on your right is *Cerro Gordo* itself, which in Spanish means "fat hill". On its face is an enigmatic white building, with several smaller structures surrounding it. Often mistaken for a church, it was built by a watchmaker, Kurt Schramm, as his home in the 1940s and 50s. It is built entirely of salvaged materials. Schramm's son now lives in the house.

In addition to Cerro Gordo's mixture of architectural styles, you'll note such interesting touches as windmills, old-fashioned weather vanes, orchards, a mini-mosque in a field, pyramid-shaped skylights, windchimes, and an occasional colorful banner floating from a post or rooftop. On your left, shortly after leaving the park, look for a wonderful two-story house made entirely of stone. It looks as though it might have been transplanted from an English village. In reality, it was once the pig barn of a local farm.

Further down Cerro Gordo you'll find more exquisite stonework, and a small abandoned family chapel made of rock.

Abruptly you come onto the paved part of the road. As you emerge back into "civilization" you'll pass by a pastel stuccoed, low-income city housing complex. The mailboxes, all grouped together in a regimented line, stand en masse near the sidewalk. Traffic on Cerro Gordo below this point can become thick and sometimes dangerous. Be prepared to hop up on the curb to avoid a careening pickup truck.

When you reach the Gonzales Road intersection, take a left. Go downhill one block and turn left again onto Alameda. In another 3/10ths of a mile, you'll be back where you started, at Patrick Smith Park.

FORT MARCY PARK / GONZALES ROAD LOOP

This is a pleasant, hilly 4.5-mile loop that will treat you to Artist Road, a part of Santa Fe that was developed before the "boom" that began in the late sixties and has been going on ever since. A beautiful little street which you'll be hearing more about later, Artist Road is an interesting sidelight in Santa Fe history, and it runs near the site of earthen-bermed Ft. Marcy, the American citadel that loomed over the city following the war with Mexico. Basically, today's walk goes from the city's new recreation complex, up the Ski Basin road, along the winding hills of Gonzales Road and back to the rec complex via Palace Avenue and Paseo de Peralta. A couple of landmarks you'll pass are the Cross of the Martyrs and the large, pink Masonic Temple. The Gonzales Road stretch of this walk is dusty and often hot in summer: wear tough shoes and take water.

Begin at the Fort Marcy Complex community building. Not only is there ample parking, but also restrooms and water fountains. It is on Washington Avenue, a couple of blocks north of Paseo de Peralta. There may or may not be a sign visible. The large recreational complex and park that you see today are vastly different from what existed on this land through the late 1970s. Many people remember Mager's Field as a grassy oval, circled by a dirt track and bordered on one side by bleachers. Today one sees a neat,

View from Cerro Gordo Road

spacious lawn leading up to a large, modern adobe-colored sports building.

Other than the St. John's College track, Mager's Field once boasted the only track in town which was truly available to the public. A rather busy place back then, it was the scene of high school athletic training, events sponsored by the Santa Fe Striders, activities of a young running group called the Santa Fe Stars, and many a lone novice jogger plodding through those first arduous miles. The best runners in town could be found at one time or another sprinting through 440's, 220's or 110's on the grass.

The track is now gone, and in its stead is the large, indoor sports complex. It helps serve the city's expanding hunger for recreational facilities. The Fort Marcy complex offers a gym, raquetball courts, an indoor pool and classes in jazzercise, aerobics and karate. Recently, a running course which also includes fitness exercises has been added. Inexpensive memberships can be purchased by the month or the year. This is also the start-finish point for the annual Fowl Day Run, a pre-Thanksgiving race which collects food for those in need.

Begin today's walk by heading out the center's broad driveway. Carefully cross busy Washington Avenue and go up Artist Road, the ascending street just across from the complex. You will have sidewalk only part of the way, so it's best to keep to the left to spot oncoming traffic. Artist Road becomes Hyde Park Road, commonly called the "Ski Basin Road", further up the grade. During winter months, you'll encounter dozens of cars with skis on top, as well as youthful ski hitchikers at the corner of Sunset Street and Artist Road. The main attraction of Artist Road, however, is the beauty and variety of the homes on either side.

There is a unique quality about Artist Road that seems to be the result of its age, its population density and its natural situation. Santa Fe is known for houses and entire residential areas perched on hills, but in many of the hillier areas you'll see patches of weeds or natural vegetation around the houses. Here on Artist Road, you find both the hills and well-tended gardens. There's also a wide variety of house styles: stucco with turquoise trim, softly-rounded adobes with deep *portales*, two-story wooden homes with balconies. Fences also are diverse: some are of round stones, others are adobe with archways and peek-through spaces, still others are fashioned of wrought-iron grillwork, reminders of Santa Fe's strong Hispanic tradition. There are also several juniper pole coyote fences. On summer nights you may hear coyotes howling in the nearby mountains, but it's been a long time since they've roamed the town. The fences are

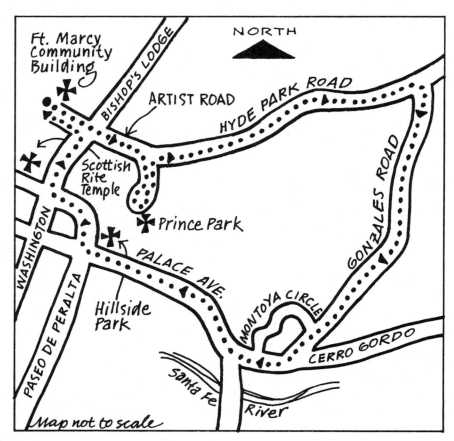

NORTH

Ft. Marcy
Community
Building

BISHOP'S LODGE

ARTIST ROAD

HYDE PARK ROAD

Scottish
Rite
Temple

GONZALES ROAD

Prince Park

WASHINGTON

PALACE AVE.

PASEO DE PERALTA

Hillside
Park

MONTOYA CIRCLE

CERRO GORDO

Santa Fe
River

Map not to scale

used nowadays simply because people like the look.

In summer, the lawns inside these enclosures are some of the greenest in town, and flower gardens abound. The age of an area is revealed in part by the size of its trees: well-developed poplars, blue spruce, aspen, pinons and firs enhance this neighborhood.

Make your way steadily uphill. After you've passed by the houses along Artist Road, you'll notice Fort Marcy Compound looming on the righthand side. It is one of the original condominiums in a city where there are now dozens. Across the street from the condo cluster, you will see a pinon-studded valley, as yet undeveloped and typical of northern New Mexico's terrain.

As you reach the compound, walk in back of it for a view of where Fort Marcy used to be. Take a right at the driveway (Prince Avenue) and stroll back to an area designated the L. Bradford Prince Memorial Park. There are a few picnic tables, a modest stone monument to Governor Prince and an earthen mound. It's easy to see why this site was chosen for the city's defense. The view of Santa Fe below is unobstructed, and parties approaching the city from north and south could be seen while still a long ways off. Walk over to the edge of the hill to see the large white tip of the Cross of the Martyrs. The cross commemorates the priests who were killed during the Pueblo Revolt of 1680. During Santa Fe's annual Fiesta, a candlelight procession leads from St. Francis Cathedral up to the Cross of the Martyrs, where a solemn service is held. An occasional artist may be at work here, easel and paints balanced on the rocky ground. More often than not, however, the park seems deserted.

Now retrace your steps to Artist Road and turn right. The road continues up through the foothills to Hyde State Park (eight miles distant) and Santa Fe Ski Basin. You won't be going that far today, but you will enjoy a lovely panorama of the Sangre de Cristos straight ahead as you pass through a stretch that is fast being built up with new housing complexes. Despite rapid development, however, it still maintains a pastoral feeling. The natural hills and the looming mountains combat any impression of urban sprawl.

Continue on uphill all the way to Gonzales Road which will intersect on your right. You'll want to pause more than once to look back at the mountains that define Santa Fe's southwestern skyline: the large rounded hump of the Sandias, the jagged outline of the Jemez, and the prominent Tetilla Peak. It is just about a mile to the Gonzales Road turnoff.

At the sign for Gonzales Road, turn right into another attractive residential area. Lawns for these homes adhere more to the "natural look" than those you observed on Artist Road, reflecting the Santa Fe of the 1970s and 80s. Here you'll see a more consistently modern Santa Fe style of architecture: a large number of solar features as well as the use of native plants such as chamisa and *cholla* cacti. As you walk along Gonzales you will see the Sun and Moon mountains ahead and to your left. Sunmount is the larger hill, Moon Mountain slightly smaller and further south. Both of these pinnacles are favorite hiking spots near St. John's College.

The first part of Gonzales Road is fairly flat. After about half a mile, you'll begin a gentle curve and descent. Look up on the ridges and slopes of the Sangre de Cristo foothills to get an idea of this area's burgeoning. Now dotted with new homes, the entire area around Gonzales Road was mostly pinon forest as recently as the mid 1970s. Now, like much of Santa Fe's outlying area, it is infiltrated with new roads and houses. All, however, is not new. There are a few homes surrounded by old funky cars and ramshackle "additions" — a refreshing break from so much trendiness.

After you've been on Gonzales Road for a bit under a mile, you'll dip down again and then back uphill. At the top of the rise, you'll pass by Las Vistas townhouses on the left. Just after this complex, shooting off to the right, is Montoya Circle, a small pocket of old adobes. Shortly you'll be on pavement again. Just beyond Montoya Circle, take a sharp right downhill onto Cerro Gordo Road. There's a sidewalk on the left side only and as you stroll down it you'll be overlooking the flat rooftops and soft adobe forms of the old Field Compound, built as an estate for the Marshall Field family of Chicago.

Just one block further and Cerro Gordo ends at Palace Avenue. Turn right onto Palace. In contrast with the bare, open feeling of Gonzales Road, Palace is tree-lined, walled, and shady. Stay to the right and enjoy the old, deep red brick sidewalk. Glossy with age, the walk dips and swells from the growth of roots and the buckling of time. Another indication of Palace Avenue's relative oldness is the size and majesty of its trees. The older homes along this street, Anglo-built mansions from early in this century, are adorned with vines and bushes. As you run or stroll Santa Fe, you'll come to appreciate these more established neighborhoods, and to recognize them by the diversity of their homes as well as their lush vegetation.

Palace Avenue is one of these verdant stretches. In spring and summer, many flowers are in evidence. Nowhere seems exempt from the condominium craze, and you'll find a few of them here as well. But there is also a nice balance of homes that are ordinary, not posh. As you start along Palace, you'll see a tiny neighborhood grocery, as well as an adobe-style laundromat, near the intersection with Cerro Gordo.

As you near the Plaza via Palace Avenue, you'll pass by brick houses with pitched roofs, large walled estates set back from the road, intriguing gates and courtyards—a delightful medley. It is this very miscellania that distinguishes Santa Fe's older areas from newly-built, rather uniform Pueblo-style condominium "cities". You'll pass the Francesca Hinijos House, with its red pitched roof and deep-set *portal,* the elegant stone Episcopal Church of the Holy Faith (over a century old), and see the white and yellow house of early Santa Fe merchant Willi Speigelburg, now an office building. The last-mentioned landmark stands at the northwest corner of Palace and Paseo de Peralta, and here you turn right at the light signal.

Wend your way north along Peralta, passing more houses of varied styles and large old trees. You'll walk by some old brick homes with pitched roofs. Nestled on the corner of Peralta and Marcy Street, on your right, you'll come to a charming little triangle of land designated Hillside Park. Here are large trees and picnic tables, an inviting spot for a brief rest. The park is bordered on the other side by Hillside Avenue, which blends into Paseo de Peralta on the right.

Just beyond Hillside Park, and topping the Fort Marcy hill that you explored earlier, you'll see the white Cross of the Martyrs looming overhead. A locked gate bars entrance to the path that winds up the hill to the cross. At Fiesta time, the gate is opened to the candlelight procession. Anyone can join in. Across from the hill are a number of small, older houses with grassy, fenced lawns. Proceed along Peralta, following its leftward curve, until you reach the moorish-style Scottish Rite Temple. Here take a right on Washington Avenue. Just a few short blocks will take you back to the Fort Marcy-Mager's Field recreation complex and your point of origin.

Bridge over the Arroyo, Fort Marcy area.

Santa Fe's running scene is alive and well. The Santa Fe Striders running club welcomes both local and visiting runners, and there are several major races held from June through September. In June or July, the Striders hold the Santa Fe Run-around, a 10-kilometer tour of the city. On Labor Day weekend, the Santa Fe Fiesta Council, as part of the city's annual Fiesta, holds the Old Santa Fe Trail Run. This run has both five- and ten-kilometer divisions. Then, toward summer's end, local merchants host the popular five-kilometer Women's Run. All these races begin and end on the Plaza. The Striders hold weekly fun runs on Wednesday afternoons, again from the Plaza. Starting time varies from 5:00 to 6:00 p.m., earlier in the winter and later during summer months. The best way to find out about these weekly runs is just to be there slightly before they begin.

A very unique cross-country event, the Fowl Run, is held in mid-November to benefit needy families. Beginning and ending at the Fort Marcy Complex baseball field, the five-kilometer course takes runners through arroyos and hills. Instead of a registration fee, participants are asked to donate $3.00 worth of food. The Salvation Army distributes these contributions to families at Christmas time.

Santa Fe's lovely climate and scenery invite runners out at all times of day, year-round. Though it is done by a daring few, running at night is not advisable. During even the coldest winters, there is usually a warm, sunnier period of day from 11 a.m. till about 2 p.m. When ice and snow make running downright unpleasant, many local runners cross-country ski in the arroyos.

When using this wintertime substitute for running, a reliable way to clock your mileage is to pick out an area that you know is a mile and see how long it takes you to ski it. Thereafter, use this time as your mileage index. For example, if it takes you 14 minutes to cross-country ski one mile, and you go out for two hours, you'll know when you return that you've covered about 8½ miles. (Simply divide 120 minutes by 14.) Of course, you can use this formula for running as well.

Hills are not the only challenge you'll encounter running in Santa Fe. Running at 7,000 feet, if you're from a lower clime, requires some adjustment. Build up your mileage gradually—don't begin with a lengthy run. If you're breathing too hard, slow down and walk for awhile. Because of the sun's intensity, you should prepare with sunscreen lotion, sunglasses and a lightweight cap—even if they are not part of your usual running routine.

Some basics to keep in mind: Wear running shoes

with a good, firm foundation and heel base. You'll need substantial support for Santa Fe'a irregular terrain and dirt roads. If you find yourself running on a road shoulder that falls off at an extreme angle, alternate roadsides. Always seek out the flattest part of the available running area.

Before embarking, be sure to stretch thoroughly. Not calesthentics, but rather long, slow yoga-type postures that work to lengthen the muscles in the backs of your calves and thighs. It is equally important, if not more so, to stretch after you run.

Remember to relax. Let your arms swing naturally, not too close to your body, and keep your body in an upright position. Breathe in that wonderful, clear Santa Fe air, look ahead toward sky or mountains— stride out and enjoy!

ST. CATHERINE'S CROSS-COUNTRY RUN

The three-mile cross country route at St. Catherine Indian School is often considered one of the best such courses in New Mexico. Located in Santa Fe's hilly northeastern sector, the well-worn running path circles the campus, climbs high atop a pinon-covered ridge that overlooks Rosario Cemetery, winds down a fairly steep hill into an arroyo and ends up where it begins, at the school's track. Because the route is short, you may well be tempted to under-estimate its difficulty. Each spring, when the school hosts its annual St. Catherine's Fiesta Fun Run, racers who haven't pre-run the course are often astonished at the challenge. The two trophies I've brought back from this annual fun run are among my most cherished and hard-earned.

To reach St. Catherine's, drive to 801 Griffin Street on the north side of Paseo de Peralta. Before embarking, I recommend you to take a tour of the picturesque campus. (You might not feel like it afterwards!) Chances are, if you ask at the main office, someone from public relations will gladly guide you about. But you can just stroll around on your own. Students are generally very courteous and helpful, and visitors most welcome.

St. Catherine's history dates back nearly 100 years. A project of Katharine Drexel, a Philadelphian of considerable wealth, the school first opened its doors in 1887. In 1891, Miss Drexel became a nun and founded

St. Catherine's Indian School

the Congregation of the Sisters of the Blessed Sacrament. In 1894, she sent the first group of Sisters to St. Catherine's and the education of young American Indians began in earnest.

Katharine Drexel, heiress to multi-millions, enabled the school to operate on interest from the family fortune until 1955. Her death at age 97 brought an end to this arrangement. What might have been a huge endowment for the school thereupon evaporated. However, through the efforts of the Congregation of the Sisters of the Blessed Sacrament, the school rose to prominence. This order has also founded 25 elementary schools, three high schools, and Xavier University in New Orleans.

Today, the focus of St. Catherine's High School has changed considerably. More and more, both Anglo and Hispanic students are being recruited. Instead of being purely a boarding school for Indians, St. Kate's is also a day school, and at least 15% of its enrollment is non-Indian.

The campus itself is immaculately kept. A strong work ethic operates at the school, and even today students are responsible for some of the cleaning and maintenance. For the most part, the campus buildings are lovely old adobe and brick edifices. If you have time during your pre-run investigation, visit the school's "Ed O'Brien Room". An unusual mural painted by Edward O'Brien in the 1960s dominates one wall. Spaniards, Indians, Southwestern farmers, the Incas and Mayas, and Catholic personages are all part of a fascinating montage. North, South and Central America are represented around the mural's focal point, Our Lady of Guadalupe. Adjacent to the mural room is a lovely, quiet chapel where students attend mass each Sunday.

Colorful artwork is found everywhere on campus, both on building exteriors and in the classrooms and administrative buildings. The walls of the main school building are painted with depictions of St. Francis Cathedral, the churches at Santa Clara, Acoma, Santo Domingo and Laguna. Maria Martinez, the internationally famous San Ildefonso potter was a graduate of St. Catherine's. Every year the school holds Christmas and spring art shows to exhibit the work of promising young art students.

Another highlight of your tour should be the small but impressive school library. In addition to the collection of some 10,000 books, you will see furniture and bookshelves with engraved and painted designs. Both the furniture and the decorations were created by students during the 1930s.

After your tour of the campus, walk beyond the classrooms and dormitories to the baseball field. Located to the right of the campus buildings, the

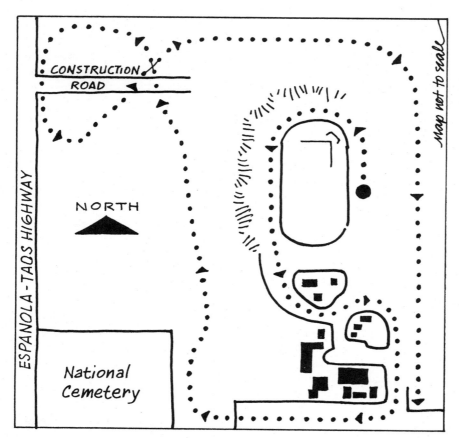

CONSTRUCTION ROAD

ESPANOLA - TAOS HIGHWAY

NORTH

National Cemetery

Map not to scale

baseball field is found at the end of a short, curving dirt road. It is here that the St. Catherine's cross-country race begins and ends. The course which you'll be undertaking is all ups and downs, so it is wise to stretch well before you start to run. If you want to make sure the course is at least three miles, you'll need to begin and end with a lap around the field.

Set your stopwatch before starting out, if you have one. I find it's often fun to treat a short run as a race, even though you are just racing with yourself. Go once around the field and then head out and down the main driveway to the campus. At the bottom of the driveway, take a sharp right, and head up toward the ridge which looms ahead. Now outside the school grounds, you'll be running along the southern border of St. Kate's—past the senior high class building, the office and the junior high. Keep wending your way right. To your left is Rosario Catholic Cemetery and Santa Fe's National Cemetery. At the far edge of the campus, perched atop a craggy hill, is a building which serves as both convent and dormitory. When you see this landmark, take another right-hand turn and run up a rather steep hill. There is a well-worn path all along the way: Just follow it and you won't wander far off track.

The ridge which overlooks the tombstones of Rosario Cemetery to the left and the school to the right is the loveliest part of this run. The course includes several steep ravines which may strain your quadraceps, so unless you're accustomed to hill running you should take it easier than usual. If you feel yourself tightening up, it's a good idea to pause as necessary to stretch. Even if you're timing yourself, the brief time out when needed will do more good than harm. In my own recreational running here, a pause for stretching has prevented many a pulled muscle or sore tendon.

The ridge, which parallels St. Francis Drive (down on your left), dwindles out rather suddenly. Veer left, go downhill, and then turn and run in the opposite direction (back towards town) along the highway. There's always a lot of traffic here, but the shoulder is wide and you'll be running facing the traffic. The stretch along the highway is not as scenic as the rest of today's course, but it is over quickly. After roughly a tenth of a mile, you'll see a dirt construction road on the left. About a tenth of a mile after you see this road, turn sharply left and head back uphill through the pinons to the ridgetop path you just left. When you hit the path, turn left and continue for another tenth of a mile.

When you see a rutted path veering downhill on your right, take it and scramble downhill to the arroyo which constitutes the last part of the fun run. Keeping the basic pattern of the course in mind will help avoid getting lost: Remember that you're running a big rectangle around the school's perimeter, with the added extras of the St. Francis Drive section, the long driveway into the school and two circuits of the baseball diamond.

Shortly after the turnoff from the ridge, you will reach a sandy arroyo. Take a right-hand turn here, and continue running the arroyo all the way back to the school's entrance. Though flat, the arroyo bottom offers its own kind of challenge. Naturally, you will sink down further into sand than dirt, and it takes more exertion just to raise your feet. If you keep the same pace that you've had for the first two-thirds of the race, you may find yourself running out of breath. If this is your intention, fine. But remember that while running in sand is an excellent ankle-strengthener, it can be somewhat dangerous. (If you haven't done arroyos before, first read my **Running the Arroyos** chapter.)

Now the arroyo heads back alongside the field where you first began. At the arroyo's end, you'll find yourself at a road. Turn right, and then right again through the stone gateway to the school. Run up the drive, then onto the dirt road to the baseball field. Once there, do a final lap around, and you're finished with the 3.1 miles. If you've been timing yourself, remember to stop your watch.

The hardy may want to make this a ten-kilometer circuit. After you have run around the field, go back down the drive and repeat the circuit. This 6.2-mile distance is included in the St. Catherine's Fiesta Runs each April. You might want to do the 3.1 mile course on a couple of occasions, take in a few longer runs, and then tackle this double course. It's undoubtedly the most challenging ten-kilometer race the city has to offer.

DEDE'S BRIDGE RUN

The bridge run takes you through the oldest parts of Santa Fe. It begins on the Plaza and follows closely along the Santa Fe River. It's a loop of about three miles. Devised by long-time runner Dede Collins, the route is best on an early, traffic-free morning. If you're an early morning person, you'll find this a perfect run for dawn. Later in the day it will still be pleasant, but much of your enjoyment may be interrupted by watching for cars. The beginning and end of the run take you close to St. Francis Cathedral, and during summer months you can see the sun coming up directly behind the church. In winter, when the sun is further south, the sunrise is still glorious, if not quite so dramatic.

Dede called this route the "bridge run" because along it there's the potential to cross over the Santa Fe River five or six times. There are a number of bridge styles here, from small narrow single-laners to large concrete and asphalt constructions. (It could just as appropriately be dubbed the riverside run as it follows along the Santa Fe River banks very closely.) An added treat is the inclusion of the *Barrio de Analco* section of the city, one of our oldest and most historic.

The bridge run is quite flat and good for making a fast time. During the first mile or so, don't worry if you find yourself running on a different side of the river than specified in this chapter. Feel free to follow

Eli Levin '86

your impulse: cross the river or not, as you like. It will still add up to about three miles. And no matter which side of the river you run, this run is one of the lovliest in Santa Fe. Because there are trees all along your way, it is especially pleasurable during summer months.

Begin on the south side of the Plaza and head east toward the facade of St. Francis Cathedral, which you can see at the end of East San Francisco Street. At the intersection you'll turn right onto Cathedral Place. A trip back later to the cathedral is a must, but as you pass by initially, note the majestic Mid-Romanesque style of the church and its two blunted, slightly asymmetrical towers. A statue of Archbishop Lamy dominates the courtyard in front.

The cathedral site has a history that long predates 1869, when Archbishop Lamy set the first stone of his dream church. Following his arrival in Santa Fe during August of 1851, Lamy yearned to build a church more elegant than the giant adobe *Parroquia* which stood at the site. He may have been homesick for his native France. At any rate, he ordered the *La Parroquia* torn down to make way for an elegant cathedral in the European tradition of the Middle Ages. He employed the skills of architects from Italy and France and work by European masons. Materials were for the most part New Mexican. Most of the stone that was used came from the Lamy Junction area south of the city.

The community of Santa Fe was very much involved with the building of the cathedral. An 1869 issue of *The New Mexican* lists local donors who gave money toward its construction. The Spiegelbergs, a prominent Jewish merchant family, were reported to have given an "astonishingly generous" $500.

Apparently the archbishop had brought a sick Levi Spiegelberg into Santa Fe when the latter's wagon party was on the verge of leaving him in a trapper's cabin. Though Spiegelberg was suffering from a form of dysentery, his companions feared cholera and wanted him out of the wagon. Lamy happened along just in time. He took Spiegelberg into his care and saw that he got back home to Santa Fe, and a warm friendship later developed between the two.

Lamy's close relationships with Santa Fe's Jewish families gave rise to an interesting and persistent legend about the decoration on the cathedral facade. Some claim a portion of it bears a resemblance to the Hebrew Star of David. As conjecture has it, another Jewish merchant, Abraham Staab, destroyed some promissory notes from the archbishop in exchange for an active part in the design of the cathedral. Could the supposed "Star of David" have been added to the cathedral as an expression of gratitude? Historians point out that it was not uncommon for Roman church-

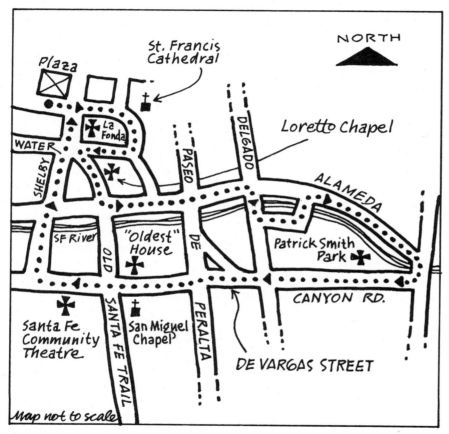

NORTH

Plaza

St. Francis
Cathedral

Loretto Chapel

La Fonda

WATER

SHELBY

PASEO

DELGADO

ALAMEDA

SF River

"Oldest"
House

DE

OLD

Patrick Smith
Park

CANYON RD.

SANTA FE TRAIL

Santa Fe
Community
Theatre

San Miguel
Chapel

PERALTA

DE VARGAS STREET

Map not to scale

es to utilize Hebrew inscriptions in their decor; and after all, Jesus of Nazareth was Jewish.

Another Santa Fe landmark looms large as you embark on this run. At the southeast corner of the Plaza, where Shelby Street meets East San Francisco, and covering the block up to the cathedral, stands the famous hotel, La Fonda. As you run by, reflect for a moment on the romance of this historic locale. *Fonda* means inn or tavern. This site has been a hotel/tavern/inn at least as long ago as 1822 when the Santa Fe Trail first opened, and possibly a lot longer. In journals and diaries of Santa Fe Trail days, La Fonda is often mentioned as the meeting place at the end of the trail. By 1877 the building at this corner was called The Exchange Hotel; it was described by *The New Mexican* as an "unimposing one-story flat."

Following World War I, The Exchange was demolished, and the site lay vacant for a time. In 1926 the land was purchased by the Fred Harvey interests, and work began on the present La Fonda. It was enlarged in 1929, 1950, and another expansion is taking place now across from the cathedral. La Fonda has seen guests from around the world, served as movie headquarters, and has long been a cosmopolitan gathering place for artists and literati. A world-famous hotel, it now also houses shops, lounges and restaurants. During Territorial days, La Fonda was known as an "in place" for monte, faro, roulette and other games of chance—including political intrigue.

Your run circles around the back of La Fonda. Turn right at narrow Water Street, and left a block later on Old Santa Fe Trail. Run past Loretto Chapel and the Inn at Loretto on your left. You're now at East Alameda. Cross Alameda and turn left onto a gravel walk. It's parallel to Alameda, and runs beside the river.

This is the beginning of a path you'll follow for about half a mile. The composition varies, from the gravel which you initially encounter to flat stones and dirt in places. This shaded, convenient pedestrian artery will enable you to meander along the river and through a part of the heart of town while safely out of traffic. Remember, you're heading east, toward the foothills, with East Alameda on your left.

Running close to the river gives you a firsthand view of the stonework that lines both sides of the river channel. The oldest hand-set stone parts were, like so many fine public projects, built by the Works Progress Administration in the 1940s. Today this often picturesque retaining structure also includes large concrete slabs as well as round stones bound with fence wire. The depth of the riverbed, along with the massiveness of the retaining wall, give a hint of how mighty the Santa Fe River can be during heavy runoffs—

and how formidable it must have been before it was dammed up.

The first bridge crossing you come to is at the intersection of Old Santa Fe Trail and Alameda, right when you first reach the gravel path. Up just a short way is another bridge—a wide affair that crosses over the river to El Castillo retirement center. In summer, the grass along this part of the run is particularly lush. All the bridges offer an invitation to cross, and you just might give in to the temptation.

In another tenth of a mile, still proceeding east along East Alameda, you'll pass the broad Paseo de Peralta bridge. On your left is a new hotel and a complex of shops developed from an old home and a set of single-story apartments. The pattern is typical of Santa Fe in recent years. A fascinating bit of World War II history occurred at this site. In 1945, at what was then called the Castillo Bridge, Klaus Fuchs, a member of the British mission to the Manhattan Project, met Harry Gold, a contact for David Greenglass. It was here that Fuchs leaked detailed information about the implosion bomb to Gold.

After the Peralta bridge, your riverside ramble will take you by scattered picnic tables which are part of Santa Fe River State Park. To your left along East Alameda, you'll see homes of various sizes and descriptions.

The Delgado Street bridge, next on your route, comes at about the half-mile mark. Cross this bridge to the south side of the river, and continue along "the other Alameda", the unpaved lane that runs parallel to East Alameda, but on the other side of the river. This bit of Santa Fe eccentricity is also considered Alameda, even though there's a gulf between it and the paved street. On this opposite bank, you'll get an even clearer look at the stonework that walls the riverbed. And, when there's been enough snow for a good spring runoff from the mountains, you'll be treated to a series of small but charming waterfalls.

Keep running on this side until the road narrows and you spot a narrow wooden bridge. This signals the end of "the other Alameda". Traverse the bridge to get back to the paved side. Turn right and continue east. There'a a path for just a bit of the way, and then you'll have to run on the road itself. It's spacious enough here to temporarily disregard the running-against-traffic rule, if you choose. But do keep an eye and ear attuned for cars approaching from behind.

There's a stop sign where Palace crosses East Alameda—and another bridge. Continue east on Alameda, past Smith Park, which fronts along the river to your right.

When you reach the end of Alameda you'll be at the confluence of several roads, including Camino

Cabra and mysterious Camino Pequeno. Cross over the large concrete bridge on your right. Once over the river, take a sharp right again onto Canyon Road. You've now switched back and you're heading west on the opposite side of the river.

You might find it interesting, as you run down Canyon Road, to try to imagine the way it was in the 1950s. There would not have been the smooth, fairly predictable footing you find today. Instead of firm asphalt, Canyon Road was often a mud quagmire in the spring and a dustbowl in the summer. Authentic and colorful though it may have been, many inconvenienced citizens felt that paving was in order. Like many proposed civic changes in Santa Fe, to pave or not to pave became a hot issue. A loud protest arose. Traditionalists rallied against converting the ancient thoroughfare from dirt to a hard surface. *The New Mexican* reported countless fiery arguments in city council meetings. There are colorful photos of artist Tommy Macaione voicing laments over the proposed Canyon Road conversion. In the end, "progress" won and the road was paved. Ironically, the curbing made the road even narrower, necessitating one-way traffic up to the Camino del Monte Sol intersection, and sidewalks are narrow, treacherous, and frequently non-existant.

In addition to shops and studios, you'll see new condominiums along Canyon Road. Sometimes new yet often constructed from the shells of older buildings, they reflect a trend that can be seen all over the city. Like the paving of Canyon Road, condominiums have become a heated local issue. The sleek new dwellings can be seen, cosmetically, as an upgrading. Proponents of preservation, on the other hand, argue that the new developments lack character and individuality. Whichever way you look at it, Canyon Road still has more than enough of the old to retain its fascination. Here are such landmarks as the Borrego House, now a restaurant; the Olive Rush Studio (used as the Quaker meeting house); El Zaguan (a gracious old apartment complex); and the old brick First Ward schoolhouse.

Toward the bottom of Canyon Road, just a block before it reaches Paseo de Peralta, you should veer left and enter narrow East De Vargas Street. In a very short block, you'll reach Paseo de Peralta. Cross this busy thoroughfare carefully, and then run the continuation of East De Vargas. You'll see the side of the round Territorial-style Capitol Building to your left, the Sangre de Cristo mountains to your right and back. You'll pass a small street named Orchard Drive, a reminder of the time, not so long ago, when farming was part of city life, even here.

You're now running through the *Barrio de Analco,*

one of the oldest sectors of original Santa Fe. Historians differ, but there is a popular theory that in the 1600s Mexican Tlaxcalan Indians resided here. The site may also have been populated by Santa Fe's original residents, the Indians of the pueblo of *Ogopoge*. *Analco* literally means "the other side of the river". *Barrio* means neighborhood or community.

Indian inhabitants built the original walls of San Miguel Church, generally credited as being America's oldest chapel. You pass along its right flank just before East De Vargas crosses Old Santa Fe Trail. Its history is lengthy and dramatic. San Miguel Church is a monumentally sculpted adobe structure. During the Revolt of 1680, San Miguel was nearly destroyed. It was reconstructed in the 1690s and a belfry tower was added, probably in 1830. Some natural cause, perhaps an earthquake, felled it in 1875, taking with it a 780-pound bell. The massive bell, itself the topic of many stories, was never hung again, but it is displayed prominently in the church's gift shop for visitors to see and touch today.

Across the street from the church is the alleged "Oldest House". The building is partly occupied by an Indian pottery and jewelry shop. One room at the heart of the Oldest House is open for viewing. The claim of ultimate antiquity is open to question; for instance, the walls are of adobe bricks, and making mud bricks was a technique the Spanish introduced to the Indians no earlier than 1598. The Pueblo people formerly "puddled" adobe mud to form the walls of their dwellings.

Many occupants supposedly resided here: priests, Indians, traders and even *brujas* (witches). Alice Bullock describes one bruja story in her book, *Living Legends of Santa Fe County*. In the 1880s, legend would have it, two brujas in the house were frequented by prominent citizens for advice and potions. The brujas possessed cures, charms and drugs that could make erring husbands return, captivate sweethearts or make rivals take ill and even die.

As the story goes, two young men were once in love with the same girl and consulted the brujas separately. Afterwards, the girl chose one of the suitors over the other. The rejected swain was so distraught that he demanded a refund from the brujas. When they refused, a fight ensued and the young Spaniard was beheaded. Now, says the tale, each year on the day of his death, the rejected lover's head rolls down Old Santa Fe Trail in a spirit of revenge and anger. In an effort to find justice, the head supposedly goes toward the Palace of the Governors.

After you pass the Oldest House and San Miguel Church, carefully cross Old Santa Fe Trail and continue on the last stretch of East De Vargas. You'll see an interesting apartment house made entirely of stone, more condos, the Roque Tedesqui House (once owned by an Italian trader of that name), and an old Territorial-style home that once belonged to Gregorio Crespin. Both of these homes have been plaqued by The Historic Santa Fe Foundation. Exact dates are unclear, but the Tedesqui house appears on records as far back as 1842, and the Crespin House dates back to at least 1747.

Across from the Tedesqui House is Santa Fe Community Theatre's building. The oldest legitimate theatre in New Mexico, it has been in operation for 61 years. The building, over 100 years old, first served as a livery stable and then as Miller's Blacksmith Shop. In the 1920s it became a garage, complete with grease-pits, and at another time an art gallery shared the space. In the late 1950s, the grease pits were floored over and it began life anew as a theatre building. The popular Fiesta Melodrama is staged here each year. Today, the Community Theatre is one of the most active theatrical groups in the city.

Before leaving the Barrio de Analco section for your final destination on the Plaza, dwell a bit on this intriguing footnote: But for the remonstrations of 24 concerned citizens two centuries ago, the Plaza area might have been moved here! According to Marc Simmons in *Yesterday in Santa Fe,* Don Juan Bautista de Anza, governor of the Spanish New Mexico in the 1770s, felt that the higher ground of the Analco area would be less subject to flooding than the original Plaza site. Some Santa Feans of that era feared moving the city center would leave their fields prey to wild animals, raiding Indians and thieves. They adamantly preferred the risk of being flooded to the consequences of having the town's hub moved to the other side of the river. Accordingly, when De Anza turned a deaf ear to their pleas, the 24 citizens went all the way to Arizpe, Sonora, Mexico, to protest to the commanding general. Thanks to them, the Plaza remained where it is today.

As you end your exploration of De Vargas Street, you'll pass the backs of the State Library, to your left, and Supreme Court Building, to your right. Right before De Vargas runs into Don Gaspar Avenue, you come to a wide cement driveway on your right that slants downhill toward the river park. Take a right here, and then cross over the picturesque stone bridge that is right next to the old Ciderpress building (now law offices). Cross Alameda and slant over to Shelby Street. Run Shelby one block to Water Street, and continue straight on past La Fonda where you'll find yourself back to your point of origin, the Plaza.

St. John's College

THE OLD SANTA FE TRAIL RUN

Of all the footraces held in Santa Fe—and they seem to be growing in number by the year, the Old Santa Fe Trail Run is the oldest. The first one took place in 1978. In the earliest years of the race, the route was never quite the same, but the race always includes part of Old Santa Fe Trail. It has attracted more local runners than any other event, and it has also drawn world class competitors like Frank Shorter, Ric Rojas and Tony Sandoval. Even during the year no sponsor could be found for the Run, it was held anyway (the Striders Running Club held a low-key "Remember the Old Santa Fe Trail Run", and the kept the tradition going). The following year, the Fiesta Council assumed sponsorship, and it has come to be one of the highlights of Santa Fe's Fiesta season in late summer.

The ten-kilometer Old Santa Fe Trail Run started out as a small event during the 1978 Fiesta, and came to be as an outgrowth of "fun runs" that were held every Saturday morning to encourage novice runners. The year before the first "official" Santa Fe Trail Run, an informal ten-mile "Fiesta Run" had taken place. When a committee formed to plan a run for tourists and nationally competitive runners as well as local people, it was decided to make the race 10 kilometers.

Choosing a route in a city where the streets and

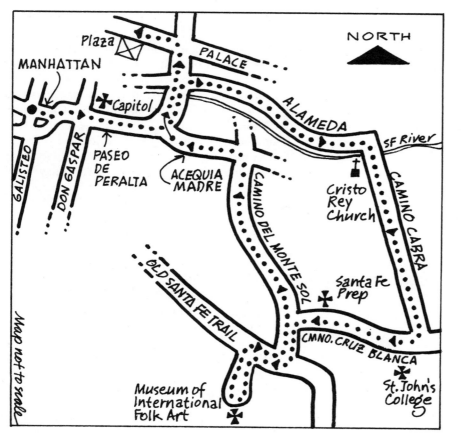

NORTH

Plaza

MANHATTAN

PALACE

Capitol

ALAMEDA

SF River

GALISTEO

DON GASPAR

PASEO DE PERALTA

ACEQUIA MADRE

CAMINO DEL MONTE SOL

Cristo Rey Church

CAMINO CABRA

OLD SANTA FE TRAIL

Santa Fe Prep

CMNO. CRUZ BLANCA

St. John's College

Museum of International Folk Art

Map not to scale

roads are hardly ever wide, straight and flat was a challenging task. After doing many miles of on-foot "running research" a committee of race enthusiasts finally traced out a circuit that measured exactly 6.2 miles: 1OK. Yet in the first six years of the race only the finishing point, the Plaza, has remained exactly the same. Variations have been added, sections deleted. The run I offer to you in this chapter is as close to the original as possible. The route offers views of residential areas and mountainous countryside. It is also one of the most challenging ten-kilometer courses you'll find anywhere.

. The original beginning for the Old Santa Fe Trail Run course was south of the State Capitol Building on Paseo de Peralta. Because Camino Cabra has been altered (later on in the route) and accordingly shortened, I am moving the start back a few tenths of a mile to the intersection of Manhattan and Galisteo streets.

During the race of '78, taking off from such a narrow spot would hardly have been feasible: 1,200 runners gathered at the start. But other than the sendoff point, you will be duplicating the course of '78, as you run the eastern curve of Peralta, swing up Alameda and Camino Cabra, traverse eastside arteries to the Folk Art Museum, then wend your way down to the Plaza via Camino del Monte Sol, Acequia Madre and Palace Avenue.

Begin a full block west of the Capitol Building, at the point where Manhattan Avenue intersects Galisteo Street. Follow Manhattan east (towards the capitol) for a short block till it ends at Paseo de Peralta. If you're doing this run for time, you'll find you will gain some speed later on. The beginning part requires a bit of winding and street-crossing, and it may slow you down. And unlike the scheduled event, the city isn't barring the streets of traffic for your personal challenge.

Take a left at Paseo de Peralta and cross Don Gaspar. You will find yourself running alongside the State Capitol, otherwise known as "The Roundhouse", or even less formally, "The Bull Ring". It is shaped roughly like the Zia sun sign (circular, with four projecting entrances), surrounded by trees, shrubs and flowers in abundance. Time, effort and that precious commodity water, have not been spared in the creation of this garden spot. The most impressive trees here are the massive willows and tall Lombardy poplars. Some say the vegetation helps hide a less-than-perfect architectural compromise. A sleek, modern Capitol design met with staunch opposition from local traditionalists. The Territorial-style bricks and white window dressing were hastily added to the plan so the building would pass muster.

At the Capitol building, cross Peralta and run along the sidewalk on the right side of the thoroughfare. On your immediate right you'll see a prominent white stuccoed building. Formerly the mansion of a prominent Santa Fe family dynasty, the Greers, this palatial structure retains a share of its original elegance. It is trimmed in red brick and fronted with a deep porch. The expansive lawn is shaded by large fir trees, and spruces. Decorative shrubs and rose bushes border the lawn, which used to extend several yards further north. The estate was truncated when Paseo was widened to four lanes in the 1960s. A small formal fish pond, now empty, is set in the center of a ring of giant boxwoods. A low white wall, with circular ironwork, borders the entire estate.

Beyond the white mansion are two handsome homes originally owned by the prominent Digneo family. Now serving as elegant office buildings, both are excellent representatives of turn-of-the-century architectural influences. Both are brick, trimmed with white and covered with ivy vines. The first one you'll pass is newer and larger. It was built around 1911. The second, directly adjacent, was constructed in 1889. Both are characterized by straight lines and a graceful understated dignity. They provide a pleasing stylistic contrast to much of Pueblo-influenced Santa Fe. They echo of the era when the Territory of New Mexico was approaching statehood at last.

A bit about the Digneo family. Carlos Digneo arrived in Santa Fe in 1880, along with his brother Michelangelo. He and other skilled stonecutters and masons worked on the construction of St. Francis Cathedral. Apparently adapting quite well to Santa Fe, the Digneos and their relatives erected many homes and buildings throughout the area. The foundation of the Digneo-Valdes house (the smaller of the two I've just described) was laid by fellow masons who were also building St. Francis Cathedral. The second owner of the house, Felipe Valdes, was married to a niece of the Digneo family. Lydia Valdes Stump, the third owner, sold the home in 1960 to a local law firm. The architectural integrity of both this house and the one next door has been carefully preserved.

Continue on Paseo de Peralta through the sometimes busy intersection with Old Santa Fe Trail, and go with Peralta's long curve to the north. You'll have a sidewalk all along. Run past the little intersection where Acequia Madre feeds into Peralta. Just beyond the curve, across to your left, is another historical home, the Jose Alarid House. Now an art gallery, this 1830s adobe has a pitched roof and white trim. It was owned by several families prominent in Santa Fe history, including Bishop Lamy. Pass the place where

Canyon Road takes of on your right and cross the wide bridge over the Santa Fe River.

Now you've reached the intersection of Peralta and Alameda. Take a right. The narrow Santa Fe River State Park, which you now find yourself running beside and through, offers grass, shade trees and a dirt footpath. You'll enjoy a bankside view of the river, now usually just a sparkling trickle but once the lifeblood of Santa Fe. Early on, its waters were directed into several man-made *acequias* (ditches) and used for irrigating cultivated fields around the city. Early in this century, Santa Feans found fishing the river an ideal Sunday outing. Nowadays, the only time fish swim in the river's waters is when the authorities to stock it for a children's "fishorama". Nonetheless, even if the river seems practically dry, it provides an oasis effect in the city's heart. The massive yet graceful cottonwoods, verdant grass and picnic tables of the river park are a welcome relief from increasing urbanization. In the winter, this park offers some of the most beautiful snowscapes to be found in Santa Fe.

Run east beside East Alameda, staying to the right for a good view of the river and the stonework along both banks. This attractive river embankment was originally constructed as part of a WPA project. The wall continues on for nearly a mile, and makes an interesting mosaic to study as you run.

After you cross the Delgado Street intersection, your running path narrows considerably and it is occasionally necessary to lean left to avoid low-hanging tree branches. Note that after the Delgado intersection that there is a dirt road paralleling your route on the other side of the river. It is, in fact, also part of Alameda—probably the only street in town divided down the middle by a river! By the time you have reached Palace Avenue, however, "the other Alameda" dies out. And so does your footpath.

Pass the Palace/Alameda junction, and cross over to the left side of the street, where you can run either on the brick sidewalk or on the pavement. The road is lighter in traffic here, so either choice is safe. Enjoy the flatness here; the course soon takes a long uphill stretch. Along this shady section of the run you'll be treated to some palatial homes on the left and the grassy fields of Patrick Smith Park on the right.

Shortly after the park ends, so does Alameda. Veer to the right on the main paved route across the river, and begin the tough uphill stretch that lasts all of Camino Cabra. This street is as scenic as it is difficult. There are several sights here to take your mind off the relentless demands of the hill. Run on the left side of the road, keeping to the sidewalk. At the very beginning of Cabra, you'll see the magnificent Cristo

Rey Church, flanked by the old Manderfield Elementary School, most recently used for Operation Headstart. The lower and upper portions of Canyon Road branch off to your right and left. The hillsides near the church are dense with houses built in a delightful hodgepodge of styles: Spanish-Pueblo, Territorial and a lot in between. Truly indigenous Santa Fe! Further up the hill, you'll run past two more elementary schools, one public (Atalaya), the other private (Rio Grande). You'll soon feel you're running in open country. At the top of your uphill stretch, nestled in the Sangre de Cristo foothills, is St. John's College.

Take an orientation to your natural surroundings. To your far left is a view of the Ski Basin and up ahead are the pinon-covered peaks known as Moon and Sun Mountains. Sun Mountain is the larger, closer peak to the right, and Moon Mountain is its smaller twin to the left. They are favorite local hiking spots which can be reached by following the arroyo behind St. John's College.

But that's for another day. For now, concentrate on your arm swing, and lifting your knees. The pumping action will help propel you up Camino Cabra. Don't push it if you're not quite used to the altitude. Remember that it's perfectly alright to slow to a jog or even a brisk walk. In Santa Fe Trail Runs of the past, I have seen runners get so weak on this hill that they've had to drop out of the race. Santa Fe's own "heartbreak hill". Be realistic with yourself and consider the altitude, the challenging grade, as well as your own training. The real joy of running comes when you can balance relaxation and refreshment with pushing yourself just a little harder. If you've never trained on hills, take this one easy.

When you reach Los Miradores condominium development, take heart. You're nearly at the top! Pass by the entrance drive to St. John's campus and then coast down about half a mile to Camino del Monte Sol. By the way, you are no longer on Camino Cabra. At the very top of the grade, Cabra turns to the west and becomes Camino de la Cruz Blanca. Stay on the left side of the road, as you'll be able to run on a dirt path over the curb for most of this section. Looking out toward Tetilla Peak and the Sandia Mountains, you should now be able to not only recover from Camino Cabra but also gain some momentum.

Pass the tennis courts, soccer field and track of St. John's College on the left and the athletic field of Santa Fe Preparatory School on the right. At Camino del Monte Sol take a sharp left. Shortly after you've turned left onto "The Camino" you'll turn *right* onto Old Santa Fe Trail. One block more and then take a left onto Camino Lejo. Go all the way to the Museum of International Folk Art, then down the short driveway on your right back to Camino Lejo. Turn right and retrace your steps until you're back at the juncture of Camino Cruz Blanca and Camino del Monte Sol. This devious little stretch, known as "the blister", was put in by the original race planners to complete the full 6.2 miles. The only good thing about it is that once you're finished, it's all either downhill or flat to the Plaza.

After the "blister", run north down Camino del Monte Sol to Acequia Madre. It's narrow here with no shoulder, so exercise caution. Even at speed you'll appreciate this enchanting and historic street and its wonderful adobe facades and walls. You'll also appreciate the absence of curbs here, which allows you to get to the side of the road quickly. When you get to Acequia Madre, turn left on it and continue on this winding downhill street. Curbs here, so you'll have to pick your way along the paving and occasional sidewalk paths. Take Acequia Madre all the way until it ends at Paseo de Peralta. There's an intersection with Garcia Street and tiny Arroyo Tenorio that may temporarily confuse you—just proceed straight ahead on Acequia one more block to the Paseo.

Take a right turn at this point and round the curve on Peralta all the way past the East Alameda intersection and on to Palace Avenue. Turn left at Paseo and Palace.

The last part of the course is a straight, downhill shot to the Plaza. The invisible finish line is where Washington Avenue crosses Palace—the southeast corner of the Palace of the Governors is where you punch your stopwatch.

Arroyos in the Bellamah area

RUNNING
THE ARROYOS

So far, this book has dealt with specific routes, mainly along streets and roads or other established paths—the tried and tested. For good reason: Santa Fe's streets are convoluted, often illogical and sometimes confusing. By directing you along clearly marked routes, I have hoped to keep you from getting lost or sidetracked. Better to spend time relaxing and admiring sights than struggling to get back to where one began. However, there is a kind of on-foot wandering that can be delightful—freeform yet safe.

I'm speaking of the arroyos. These sandy washes or dry riverbeds are found throughout Santa Fe. Except during snow, spring runoff, or late summer thundershowers, they are usually dry. Arroyos offer an interesting alternative to road running and a remarkably different natural environment within the city.

For one thing, running or walking in an arroyo gets you away from the fumes and distraction of traffic. By following an arroyo out and back, you can often explore for miles in solitude, yet without much risk of getting lost. The plant and animal life there is interesting, varied and up-close. The rocky, uneven footing of arroyos is also usually soft and cushiony, excellent for ankle-strengthening.

Best of all, you can be very solitary after running just a few hundred yards from the road. The terrain offers a closeness with the earth which, for me, always borders on the therapeutic.

Finding arroyos is simple. These not-so-hidden treasures frequently run underneath bridges or culverts, or just spur directly off a main road. Excellent arroyo runs are to be found behind St. John's College, paralleling West Alameda near the Rio Vista subdivision, in the Bellamah area, and around St. Catherine's Indian School.

The arroyo environment is sandy, serene, and filled with a surprising variety of plants and animals for those who take some moments to observe. Outcroppings of rock are frequently laced with sparkling mica or quartz and a variety of colorful lichens. Clusters of evergreen pinon and juniper compete with deciduous tamarisk, Chinese elm and an occasional cottonwood. Smaller plants include the ubiquitous gray-green chamisa, prickly pear and cholla cacti, mullein, range grasses, and wildflowers in season, such as Indian paintbrush and purple asters. Occasionally darting between the clumps of shrubbery you may see harmless little lizards, a jackrabbit or cottontail, and perhaps a prairie dog. Shiny pitch-black beetles waddle along, sticking their behinds into the air when they're aware of your presence. These harmless and comical "stink bugs" only stink when stepped on. A rattlesnake is an extremely rare sight; chances are you won't see one in a year of arroyo running. Blue pinon jays scold and dart about in the trees that give them their name; overhead, black crows soar dramatically, patiently waiting for a morsel to turn up on the arroyo floor. If you are lucky, you may even see a comical, long-tailed bird scooting along through the brush with long, rhythmic strides: The splendid roadrunner, symbol of New Mexico.

You would be wise to bring a little water, sunglasses, comfortable canvas or running shoes or walking boots. Pick a landmark where you entered the arroyo, to look for on your return to the road. Use the mountains with which you've become familiar for general orientation. If you "feel lost", remember that you usually just climb up the arroyo bank to spot a road, street or other sample of civilization.

One special word of caution about arroyo adventuring, especially in late summer. If you see thunderstorm activity in the hills, there is a chance your arroyo can become suddenly awash in a flash flood. The water comes suddenly—dry arroyo one minute, broad stream the next. Dash to the nearest bank for safety. The flash flood condition usually passes in a half hour or so. But it can be quite dramatic.

More and more local people are discovering the suitability of arroyos during winter for cross-country skiing. The vagaries of Santa Fe weather are somewhat unpredictable, and there are certainly some winters when there is hardly enough snow for in-town skiing. But the trend in recent years has been toward a few very heavy snowfalls. First snows have been arriving early, by mid-October, and there are always snowfalls in March and April. A sprinkling of snow in May is not uncommon. When there is enough accumulation, the arroyos offer very pleasant cross-country terrain. It's best to go out early after fresh accumulation. The more skied-down an area gets, the icier and less pleasant it tends to be. Local ski and sporting goods shops rent cross-country equipment.

For the daily runner, it is comforting that cross-country skiing is a perfect substitute for running. It conditions as well, and reputedly burns even more calories than running. Cross-country skiing is a splendid workout for the upper body. In running or walking, the upper body more or less "goes along for the ride," whereas in cross-country the shoulders, arms and torso are all brought into play.

Finally, road-running in ice and snow can be downright treacherous. The clearance for cars is narrowed and runners must vie for space on the road. During winter conditions, the shoulder that runners usually use can become virtually nonexistent. What's more, there is often a thin layer of ice under the snow upon which one must run. Slips and falls are a con-stant threat. An hour or two of cross-country skiing in an arroyo is a convenient substitute for the perils of running winter roads.

For the runner who likes to keep track of his mile-age, it is easy enough to log in arroyo running. I generally note the time I leave the road to follow an arroyo, go for my run, and then note the time when I return. Just divide your average mile time by the total time you spent in the arroyo to get your distance. Unless you are experienced at running arroyos, you'll probably find yourself slowing down a bit. If you feel slower, add 15 to 30 seconds to your average mile time. Remember that arroyo running demands more agility, and can tax the ankles: take it easy at first, doing no more than ten or twenty minutes. Chances are, you'll like arroyo-running so much you'll soon do more, and build your capabilities accordingly.

Alas, some of the major benefits of arroyo running are also potential drawbacks. Because the footing is changeable, it's easy to trip or sprain an ankle. Again, I advise doing short arroyo runs at first, then length-ening them. Remember that it will require more con-centration and attention to the terrain, especially at first. The more you do it, the more natural arroyo run-ning will become.

For women runners one more word of caution. Health-minded pedestrians are not the only people in the world who have found the solitude of arroyos. After a few strange encounters, I have decided not to do arroyo running alone. I either take a dog along or run with one or two human friends. If you should meet questionable characters and you're alone, you don't have much chance of attracting help without a hasty retreat to the arroyo bank.

Though I earlier stressed the natural beauty of arroyos, I failed to mention the occasional car body, washing machine or old shoe. Yes, now and then arroyos are used as trash bins. (Actually, old car bodies are sometimes thrown in deliberately to keep the banks from eroding.) If you chance upon a trashy one you find offensive, seek out another. There are still plenty of relatively unspoiled arroyos. And despite the few cautions and risks, they are rewarding to the spirit and well worth exploring.

The Sangre de Cristo Mountains

III. BIKING AROUND SANTA FE

Rabbit Road, looking toward Tetia Peak

Bicycling in Santa Fe is both scenic and exhilarating. It can also be quite a challenge. The narrowness, ruts and potholes of our roads require extra vigilance. Dangerous gratings lurk to snare your wheels. It's necessary to spot them ahead of time— trying to bike over them will end in a tire getting stuck, or worse. In most parts of town there are substantial hills and long grades. It is absolutely essential here to lock your bike with chain and padlock whenever you're not riding it. In big city terms, our traffic isn't bad, but it's still heavy enough to warrant avoiding rush hours, from 7-9 a.m. and 5-6 p.m.

On the other hand, with bicycling in Santa Fe the air is fresh and the view unparalleled. By bike, you can cover territory faster than is possible by walking or running. And if you have any tendency toward ankle or knee problems, bicycling may be healthier for you than running. When injured by overtraining, many runners substitute bicycling for running: it's undeniably easier on knees and ankles.

Mountain bikes are the best all-around bike for Santa Fe touring. They're tough enough for rutted dirt roads, and fine for asphalt pitted with potholes. Great control, light weight, efficient brakes, excellent gearing and speed. They were developed by sportsmen in California, using the best ideas from BMX bikes (especially those fat, knobby tires) and touring bikes. Mountain bikes are changing the world of adventure cycling! It's possible to rent them from local bicycle shops.

Here are a few things to remember before you start out. As with walking and running, you should equip yourself for Santa Fe's variable weather. Watch for cumulus thunderheads in summer. Remember that the temperature drops dramatically toward nightfall. We have cold winters, sunny but with low air temperatures. Wind can change your conditions during a simple outing. The air may feel quite pleasant in one direction, but harsh in another. Prepare by packing a windbreaker, extra shirt and bicycling gloves. On Santa Fe's narrow and busy streets I always recommend wearing a helmet. It adds warmth as well as protecting you in case of a collision.

The usual safety rules should be amplified a bit for local conditions. Add a rear-view mirror to your bike; some attach to handlebars, or if you don't like leaning down to see, you might find a small one that attaches to your spectacles or helmet.

As our city has grown, so have traffic problems. Allow for anything to happen at any time and be prepared for erratic or irresponsible driving. If a car turns suddenly, with no warning, prepare to swing instantly in the same direction. When biking through an intersection, stay near the center of the road, and

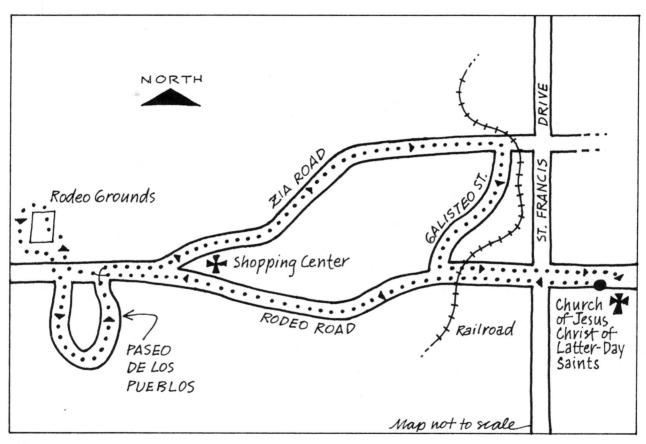

NORTH

Rodeo Grounds

ZIA ROAD

Shopping Center

GALISTEO ST.

ST. FRANCIS DRIVE

RODEO ROAD

Railroad

PASEO DE LOS PUEBLOS

Church of Jesus Christ of Latter-Day Saints

Map not to scale

use traditional arm signals for turning. Car drivers may not be looking for you, so you need to be on the lookout for them. Strive to ride in a way that's predictable.

It's quite a good idea to carry water along (you can buy tubular jugs that attach to your bike frame), and a small tool kit on longer excursions. Most bikers I've talked with take the following: a small adjustable wrench, two aluminum tire levers, a tiny screwdriver, a patch kit and a spare inner tube. If possible, attach a tire pump to your bicycle.

* * *

First, I'll mention which of the Routes for Walking are most appropriate for bicycling. Next I'll present a 7-mile loop on Rodeo Road, an easy, flat course. And finally I'll give brief directions for two longer routes devised by the old Santa Fe Bicycle Club.

The first walking path, **Plaza Area/Canyon Road/ Old Santa Fe Trail,** is fine for bikes. The trek up Camino del Monte Sol may be arduous if you aren't used to cycling hills, but the rest should be fairly easy. There are so many stops along the way you'll want to make, so be sure to have a good lock with you.

Other fine bicycling routes are the **St. John's College/Lejo Museums Walk** and the **Guadalupe Street Loop.** The remaining four walking routes include either paths or dirt roads. If you use a mountain bike, they would also be possibilities.

And now for a few selected bicycling routes...

RODEO ROAD RENDEZVOUS: This seven-mile loop, away from the hub of Santa Fe, offers relative flatness, wide streets and light traffic. It also provides a look at Santa Fe suburbia and the Rodeo Grounds. Begin your tour at the Latter-Day Saints Church on Rodeo Road. (A massive ark-like structure with a white roof, it is hard to miss.)

From the church parking lot, take a left turn out onto Rodeo Road. Wide open country here, with a view ahead of Tetilla Peak (the highest point on the horizon, and a nearly perfect anthill shape). The pinons give way to dense subdivisions as you approach the Rodeo Grounds, scene of the July Rodeo de Santa Fe. When you reach the turnoff, bike in and explore for a bit, then come back out to Rodeo Road.

Headed back toward the L.D.S. church now, you should take a right-hand turn when you reach Camino de los Pueblos Road. This is a pleasant 7/10ths of a mile that gives you a comfortable feeling of middle class suburbia, provides some variety, and insures that your route is at least seven miles. You'll follow Pueblos till it comes out again at Rodeo Road.

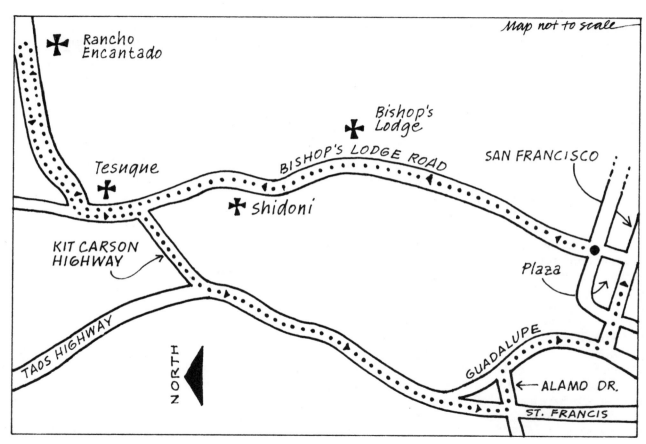

Map not to scale

Rancho Encantado

Bishop's Lodge

SAN FRANCISCO

BISHOP'S LODGE ROAD

Tesuque

Shidoni

KIT CARSON HIGHWAY

Plaza

TAOS HIGHWAY

NORTH

GUADALUPE

ALAMO DR.

ST. FRANCIS

118

Still heading back toward the church, you will be adding another loop when you get to the Y intersection at Zia Road. From Rodeo, take a left onto Zia and follow it past Ragle Park (where you'll find drinking water in summer) all the way to Galisteo Street. Take a right on Galisteo and go about half a mile until you find yourself again at Rodeo Road. Take a sharp left. Another 8/10ths of a mile, gently uphill, and you'll be back at your point of origin, the Mormon church.

ENCANTADO EXCURSION: This 19-mile out-and-back trip is hilly and dramatic. You begin in town, bike north to a famous resort, and sweep back along a busy highway. Because of traffic, a helmet is strongly advised for this trek. Also, because the route is relatively arduous, you'll want to take water along.

Starting point is the Plaza. Head north on Washington Avenue, which becomes Bishop's Lodge Road as you leave downtown. After you pass Bishop's Lodge itself, the road becomes rough and narrow. Now in the village of Tesuque, you'll pass the spectacular Shidoni Sculpture Gallery and Foundry. Keep right on the main road till you get to Kit Carson Highway. The beginning of this road is marked by a stop sign. Another mile or so beyond the stop sign you will see a turnoff to Rancho Encantado. Turn right here, bike the two miles out to the resort, and then retrace your route another two miles back.

When you once again reach the Kit Carson Highway, take a left. Bike another few miles south to Taos Highway (U.S. 84-285), the main four-lane highway leading north out of Santa Fe. This stretch offers smooth sailing, as you turn left and head south over "Tesuque Hill" and all the way down to Alamo Drive. At Alamo, take a left, keeping a sharp eye out for traffic. Another 2/10ths of a mile and you'll reach Guadalupe Street. Turn right here, bike by DeVargas Mall and go all the way to San Francisco Street. Take a left on narrow San Francisco and pedal directly back to the Plaza.

RABBIT ROAD RAMBLE: This scenic 12.2-mile course is moderately hilly, and will take the cyclist out to the scenic and open southeast side of Santa Fe. The highlight of the tour is the stretch on Rabbit Road, where you'll have a beautiful view of the mountain ranges which surround Santa Fe. Like the Encantado Excursion, it begins at the Plaza.

Go east on Palace Avenue one block and turn right at Cathedral Place. Go around the curves till Cathedral runs into Alameda, then turn right and bike two blocks till you reach Don Gaspar. At Don Gaspar, turn left and bike south through town and cross a major intersection at Cordova Road. When you reach

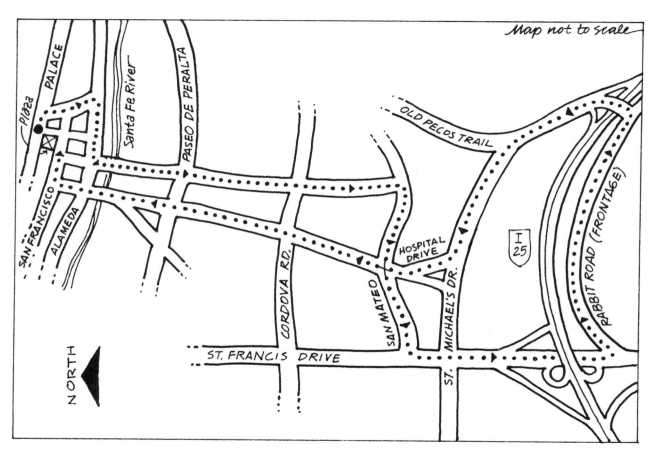

Map not to scale

Plaza
PALACE
Santa Fe River
PASEO DE PERALTA
OLD PECOS TRAIL
RABBIT ROAD (FRONTAGE)
I 25
HOSPITAL DRIVE
SAN FRANCISCO
ALAMEDA
CORDOVA RD.
SAN MATEO
ST. MICHAEL'S DR.
ST. FRANCIS DRIVE
NORTH

San Mateo Road, turn right.

You'll have been on San Mateo just under a mile when you reach the main thoroughfare of St. Francis Drive. Here, take a left and bike until you reach Rabbit Road, near the I-25 interchange. Take a left on Rabbit Road and proceed for a carefree two miles until you reach Old Pecos Trail. Rabbit is a frontage road, and usually blissfully free of traffic. Enjoy the views and the fresh, wide-open feeling here. Rabbit Road ends at the Old Pecos Trail, where you will take an immediate left.

From this point, travel north on Old Pecos Trail to St. Michael's Drive (you will need to bear to the left when the road comes to a Y at St. Michael's). Bike along St. Michael's Drive for 7/10ths of a mile till you reach Hospital Drive. Take a right on Hospital, and shortly after that another right onto Galisteo Street. Go two miles on Galisteo, till you reach San Francisco Street in the heart of the city. Take a right and proceed two blocks to the Plaza.

The Sangre De Cristo Cycle Club holds bike rides (both road and mountain) every weekend of the year. Check local bike shops for times and places. Santa Fe's annual Century Ride takes place the third weekend in May, and the Annual Hill Climb, a vertical 14½-mile rise to the Ski Basin, occurs yearly in midsummer.

Eli Levin '82

Eli Levin 82

RESOURCES

Bullock, Alice, *Living Legends of Santa Fe County*, The Sunstone Press, Santa Fe, 1978.

Celebrate! The Story of the Museum of International Folk Art, Richard Polese, ed., Museum of New Mexico Press, Santa Fe, 1979.

Comfort, Charles Haines and Mary Apolline Comfort, *This Is Santa Fe*, Santa Fe, 1955.

Hertzog, Peter, *La Fonda: The Inn of Santa Fe*.

La Farge, Oliver, *Santa Fe: The Autobiography of a Southwestern Town*, University of Oklahoma Press, 1959.

La Foya, Nicholas, *The Frontiers of New Spain*, Volume XIII, The Quivira Society, Berkeley, 1958.

Lewis B., *Oldest Church in U.S.: The San Miguel Chapel*, Santa Fe, 1968.

Myrick, David F., *New Mexico's Railroads: An Historical Survey*, Colorado Railroad Museum, Golden, Colorado, 1970.

Nusbaum, Rosemary, *The City Different and the Palace*, The Press, Santa Fe, N.M., 1978.

Old Santa Fe Today (preface by John Gaw Meem), Published for The Historic Santa Fe Foundation by the University of New Mexico Press, Albuquerque, 1966.

Shiskin, J.K., *The Palace of the Governors*, Museum of New Mexico Press, Santa Fe, 1972.

Simmons, Marc, *Yesterday in Santa Fe*, San Marcos Press, 1969.

Sussman, Aaron and Ruth Goode, *The Magic of Walking*, Simon and Schuster, New York, 1967.

"To Santa Fe by Narrow Gauge: The Denver & Rio Grande's Chili Line," Reprinted from *Colorado Rail Annual*, Special Chili Line Issue, 1969.

Twitchell, Ralph Emerson, *Old Santa Fe: The Story of New Mexico's Ancient Capital*, R.E. Twitchell, 1925.

Ungnade, Herbert E., *Guide to New Mexico Mountains*, Sage Books, Denver, 1985.

Vestal, Stanley, *The Old Santa Fe Trail*, Bantam Books, New York, 1957.

Wenzell, O.R., *Artists of Santa Fe: Their Works and Words*, O.R. Wenzell Publications, Santa Fe, 1959.